VICE COP

BILL McCARTHY

and

MIKE MALLOWE

William Morrow and Company, Inc.

NEW YORK

VICE COP

MY TWENTY-YEAR BATTLE WITH NEW YORK'S DARK SIDE

Library of Congress Cataloging-in-Publication Data

McCarthy, Bill.
    Vice cop : my 20-year battle with New York's dark side / Bill McCarthy and Mike
Mallowe.
        p.   cm.
    ISBN 0–688–08451–6
    1. McCarthy, Bill.   2. Police—New York (N.Y.)—Biography.
3. Vice control—New York (N.Y.)   I. Mallowe, Mike.   II. Title.
HV7911.M3865A3   1990
363.2'597'092—dc20
[B]   90–13365
                                                                                   Cip

Printed in the United States of America

First Edition

1 2 3 4 5 6 7 8 9 10

BOOK DESIGN BY BARBARA M. BACHMAN

ACKNOWLEDGMENTS

I've learned many things writing this book: Foremost among these insights is just how important the love of my mother and father were to my survival in the Life—for they gave me the vision of what ought to be.

The importance of having three "rabbis" or "hooks" in my life—mentors—who each happened to have a Jewish surname. They were Chief Kenneth Gussman, Chief Aaron Rosenthal, and Dr. Sam Janus. They were genuine teachers and helpers.

The importance of my two children, Christine and Billy, who gave me great guilt for my recklessness and who ultimately provided my reason for escaping the Life.

And finally, the most important thing I have learned is that my schoolteacher wife, Millie, still has plenty to teach me. Forever and eighteen days I love you. . . .

To Tony Vitaliano and the other police officers who remain on duty—thank you and be safe.

BMc.

AUTHORS' NOTE

All of the incidents and people depicted in this book are real. It is a true story. However, for reasons of both privacy and security, many of the names have been changed. Where appropriate, certain events have been slightly altered for purposes of dramatic continuity. This tinkering is almost entirely chronological and not substantive.

PROLOGUE

"You talk about being scared. This happened during the big blackout. On every street there was looting, anything they could carry. The city was out of control.

"I remember lying on the floor of the police bus that night, going to wherever they were taking us, and staying down because they were shooting out the windows. Snipers all over the Bronx.

"We pulled up at a corner and jumped out. I saw five or six guys go in through the window of a looted store. There was a kind of darkness that night like I've never experienced. No moon and, of course, all the streetlights and building lights were out. Dead black.

"I ran in behind these guys, alone.

"It was an auto parts store. As they scattered, trying to hide, going down into the basement, a couple of them bumped into an oil can display and knocked it over. First I heard the crash; I couldn't see that much. Then, I smelled this lake of oil beginning to spread all over the tile floor. I started slipping in it. Alongside another display aisle, I could make out two black guys crouched down.

"I didn't realize it at that moment, but as I went after them, I hit the spilled oil on the run and slid; I went up into the air and came down on my back. Hard. I was all wet with this stuff, covered with oil and knocked half-dizzy. When I looked up those two guys were standing over me.

"I went for my handcuffs and tried to get up on my feet, but slipped and fell again. They backed off. I could see they weren't sure if I was coming up with the cuffs or with my revolver. They also weren't sure how many of me—how many cops—there were.

"All I could do was cuff them both together and march them down into the basement while I looked around for the rest of them.

"There's four more down there; I'm sure of that. Plus my two prisoners. The only edge I have is that they probably think I'm a whole squad coming down to get them. I *couldn't* be crazy enough to be going down there by myself.

"Finally, I'm down in the basement of that store, with my gun in one hand and my flashlight in the other, holding these six guys up against the wall. *But no other cops are showing up.*

"They're beginning to look at each other with this funny expression on their faces. Like, now they *know.*

"One gun, six guys, all bigger than I am, and this is a flashlight that I've had in the trunk of my car for the last two years. Except for the beam from that flashlight you can't see a damn thing down there.

"I will never forget the absolute fear that I felt at that moment. We just stared each other down for I don't know how many minutes while I tried to figure out what to do—and I could see that they were doing the same thing as I was. To jump me or not to jump me—that was the question. We're just eyeballing each other in the darkness, waiting to see who makes the next move.

"I knew I would never be able to get all of them if they did rush me, but I had my mind made up that I wasn't going to go down by myself, either. I'd take somebody with me.

"And I'm saying to myself: McCarthy, why did you *ever* become a cop?

"And then, just as they begin to move around on me, shuffling, shifting from one leg to the other, looking to get the jump on me, the battery in my flashlight starts to go, flickering, missing. Then all of a sudden, the light goes dead.

"Dead black."

ONE

The *Life* is right now; it's instant, no past and no future. It's this moment. No other possible existence. In Vice, every player lives in the Life.

M O T H E R ' S   M A X I M

T H E   M A R Q U E E

"I can shut my eyes today and I still see the marquee—a marquee like a theater sign, with all the flashes and the little white lights running along the sides. That was the show; that was the Life and I was part of it. I was up there on that marquee.

"I see Vice.

"I see Times Square; I see the race; I see the filth; I see the massage parlors; I see the porno bookstores; I see old men trying to take small boys up to rat-trap rooms on the pedo patrol for quick, anonymous sex.

"I see all the people running—desperate, lonely people running as fast as they can just to stay in the race. In the Life.

"I see the little urchins and the little buzzards perched on shelves all over the place, all over the street. Cut purses just waiting to drop down on you, cut your pocket, steal your money. Cut your throat, take your life. If ever you tripped and fell, they'd strip you naked, steal your shoes, take your wallet and turn your pockets inside out before you knew what hit you.

"I see Forty-second Street, Eighth Avenue, the strip, the Minnesota Strip, Forty-ninth Street, the Lark Hotel; little blond whores and big black pimps.

[1]

"I see fast money and champagne ladies and goulash houses—gambling joints. I see blackjack, three-card monte. I see little, old, soft, fat guys—wiseguys—with wads of cash. I see them playing cards and getting laid and staying drunk all night.

"I see good-looking whores, great-looking whores, in apartments on Park Avenue, places where the doormen let you in.

"I see whores who don't make any bones about the fact that every man they see is a dick with a dollar sign. I see white men with money to spend on hard-faced, skinny black whores—hookers whose pupils are so dilated that their eyes, bloodshot eyes, look like they're swimming in semen. White men's semen.

"I see the basket cases, raving for a bed at Bellevue and a warm place to spend the night. I see the junkies with zombie eyes and empty hearts, their arms and legs covered with sores, with scabs, with pus you could push through to feel to their bones.

"I see the bad cops and the good cops; cops like me; tough guys with their shirts open, loud shirts; sharp guys, fast lives, good detectives. The best in New York City, which automatically makes them the best in the world.

"I see the official NYPD forms, the arrest logs, with all the neatly typed entries for crime statistics. There were specialty squads for rape and robbery and homicide, for every thing else. But there was never any single category for the crimes of Vice. There were just too many separate sins in the Life. So the police department called it *other*. Nothing else fit. That was Vice. *Other*.

"I see it all there waiting for you if you were a cop—temptation, corruption, sex, the danger. Every day it would be there. It was like going to the supermarket; walk up one aisle and down the other. Just fill up your basket. Anything you wanted, it was all marked. You knew the cost going in. It could be your career, your marriage, your pride, your soul.

"I see you paying your money and taking your shot and it would stay with you all day—the rush, the excitement, the compulsion, the feeling that you just couldn't get enough of it, enough of the Life. And all you had to do was survive. Come out alive.

"When I close my eyes today, what I see is me, Bill McCarthy, a Vice cop. I was part of it all. I understood the game and I was good at it. I belonged there. In the Life."

Bill McCarthy had disciples and enemies and absolutely nobody in between. He was the kind of cop who liked to take the first bite, the kind of cop who never stopped believing.

That made him dangerous — to the bad guys and to the New York City Police Department. When he retired on July 1, 1987 — the day that Bill McCarthy finally gave up the Life — the people who were glad to see him leave could have filled the outfield in Yankee Stadium. Most of those people were relieved; a handful of them still expected McCarthy to come back somehow and get even. He was that kind of cop.

During nearly twenty-one years on the street, mostly in the Life, in Vice, McCarthy learned that there are only two ways to look at the world — as a civilian and as a cop. The cop approaches life as one of the walking wounded, as a casualty of his line of work. He can't help himself.

The mere fact of his survival and endurance make him suspicious, aggressive, and not a little nervous in the company of noncops. It's a form of battle fatigue, only worse, because with cops, the battle is never over. Their private war goes on, and as they grow older, they become a little more desperate with each escalating danger. They can never look forward to the clean resolution that comes with the catharsis of combat. A cop's life is a limbo of blue for all eternity — no black or white, no right or wrong; their conflicts are remorselessly gray.

A long time ago, society gave cops like Bill McCarthy guns and blackjacks and expected them to serve as its bouncers. No long-winded explanations — just keep the riffraff out. Nightstick justice.

Language, even common words, had to take on new layers

[3]

of meaning for cops. "Death," for example, wasn't some inescapable consequence of the gift of life; for cops, "Death" became a wily, familiar foe, almost a friendly enemy, one who would always be there, waiting, at the beginning of every shift.

For all this they can expect low pay, lower status, and the lowest possible standard of performance from a debased criminal justice system that feeds on the husks of burned-out policemen.

McCarthy never had to shoot anybody, but people have shot at him. He's never stabbed anybody, but he's been stabbed, more than once. He's never planted a bomb, intending to do as much damage to as many people—helpless, anonymous victims—as possible, but later in his career, as the commanding officer of the NYPD Bomb Squad, McCarthy and his men were called on to locate and disarm hundreds of such bombs.

As a rule, he didn't like other cops and never really trusted them. To a large extent, that feeling was mutual. But they all knew "Mother"—part of it as in "that no good mother..." and part of it as in "Mother will never let anything bad happen to you." It became McCarthy's code name as well as his trademark.

Either way, he really was like a mother to the men he commanded, which meant that it was his responsibility to get the job done and to make sure that cops with iron balls—decent, honest, incorruptible cops—didn't get killed in the line of duty. Or caught in the merciless gears of the New York City Police Department.

Just mention that name today, "Mother," even years after his retirement, and you are likely to see some grizzled, cynical cop nod his head in immediate recognition, maybe spit or swear before he repeats the name, and then say what they almost always say, their tone a mixture of grudging respect and disbelief: "Mother—that was one crazy son of a bitch."

There is no higher compliment in the NYPD than to be labeled a madman. And Bill McCarthy was just that. Crazy.

As a package, he still makes a lasting impression with his prematurely balding head, a respectable padding of muscles, and a deceptively medium build—five feet ten and 160 pounds when he's in shape and running every day or jabbing at the heavy bag. Which he usually is.

Back in 1974, when he was just twenty-nine, at the height of his undercover roles, and as the brains behind Operation Sinbad, McCarthy appeared to be a perfectly reasonable, good-looking young cop. He deviated from the norm only in that he possessed a rock-solid upper body—developed from years in the ring—and a pair of scarred shoulders that had taken down dozens of tenement doors. But by no means was he a monster. Oddly enough, however, McCarthy always sent people away convinced that he was bigger and taller and stronger than he actually was. Call it presence—something McCarthy possessed in abundance.

There was only one physical attribute that truly set him apart. He had the coldest, deepest-set hazel eyes that any of the cops who worked for him had ever seen. Also, his face never changed expression when he was on the job; not unless he was using it to scare some poor slob.

That's when his face would twist into a gargoyle mask, those deep-freeze eyes of his popping out of his head in a steam bath of rage.

With good reason, most of his men were more afraid of him than of anybody they were likely to run into on the job. Bellowing like King Kong, he was known to pound his fists on his chest just before a fight. He used to bang his head against the wall in the bars that they raided, just to let them know that he was there, or he'd scream, "Hey, I'm gonna taste me some ear."

And they knew that he meant it. Every word. Because he *had* eaten ears before. At least that was part of the McCarthy legend. Apocryphal or not, it didn't really matter. Once, so the story went, McCarthy had bitten a pimp's bodyguard on the nose, ripped his ear half off and then chewed on it. Things like that made an impression. Especially on fellow cops.

He was acutely aware of the fact that, as a cop, his true talent lay in bleeding. McCarthy led by example—head first. As a boss, he was obsessed with the notion that no other cop's blood, real or bureaucratic, should ever be on his hands.

[5]

Police commissioners came and went, but cops like McCarthy stayed. And those commissioners, who had thirty-thousand other cops to think about, to promote, to transfer, to discipline, or to crush, if need be, were always aware of Bill McCarthy. He was not a well-kept secret. In his world, in Vice, he had come to be revered, universally, as a madman.

McCarthy *did* have a smart mouth, too, an educated mouth, and in the NYPD of his time there was always the risk of that working against you, because any cop who might be caught reading *The New York Times* in the precinct could be branded a communist or worse.

As a young man, McCarthy went on the job not even sure what the Mafia was, but by the time he left, every major organized crime family in New York had heard of Bill McCarthy. He was the crazy Vice cop who was bad for business; McCarthy cost them money. He cost them plenty.

McCarthy never took a bribe as a cop, not one dollar; but even to this day, long after his many undercover assignments, there are still people in Manhattan who believe that Bill McCarthy was the most diabolically corrupt cop who ever tried to shake them down. He was a good actor, he had to be. He was Mother.

As the head of the Pimp Squad, McCarthy lived with men and women who sold their bodies until every organ wore out. Much of his career in the Life was spent attempting to apprehend compulsive pedophiles who preyed on children—buying them, selling them, raping them, abusing them, victimizing them in every way.

When he began, only the most sophisticated criminals trafficked in drugs, and among that group only the most enterprising dealt in cocaine. But by the time he was finished every five-buck hooker, every pipe-whore who came through the Pimp Squad was hopelessly addicted to crack cocaine.

He watched as the constant dangers in the Life shifted from nightly armed struggle to near-Armageddon.

And Bill McCarthy endured. In the end, he was able to walk away from the Life with his head held high, taking more from it than he gave. It was a good run. Never once did he stop believing.

Bill McCarthy never intended to become a cop, never intended to become Mother, never dreamed of spending the best years of his life in Vice, but that's what happened, and this — told largely in his own words — is his story. It's the tale of an honest cop who lived the Life.

Like every cop, McCarthy began his odyssey as a rookie — as a frightened, well-meaning young recruit who was profoundly unprepared for the calling he was about to take up.

Long before Vice, there were the streets of Harlem and the long, bloody summer of 1966.

TWO

The *Harlem* that cops know is a butcher shop. People are just meat. Want a leg of lamb? You got a leg of lamb. Want a dead body? You got a dead body.

MOTHER'S MAXIM

HARLEM, 1966

"First of all, I *never* went to the police academy.

"I was appointed a policeman June 20th, 1966, and they immediately took us down to a tailor on Canal Street to be outfitted with two blue summer shirts and get measured for our pants. The shirts had brass buttons. I still remember that.

"Rookies were supposed to wear khaki or gray—gray for my class. But I never wore gray. None of us were ever allowed to be rookies.

"They gave us a gun in a box and sent us up to a range. We fired fifty rounds. Then they told us to put the gun back in our holster and don't ever take it out again.

"Two weeks later the pants were ready—blue pants—and I was in Harlem, in a blue uniform, like a real cop, in a riot. Summer of 1966. Two weeks later.

"It was incredible. I had never even been to Harlem in my life. I had heard about it and I knew it was a bad place. It took me fifteen minutes to drive from Queens. I paid twenty five cents to go over the Triborough Bridge, right up the main drag and get off at 135th Street and all the time I'm saying to myself,

Jesus Christ, fifteen minutes and a quarter, and I can go from an Irish Catholic neighborhood where everybody looks out for everybody else, to this. If these people ever find out that they can pay a quarter and go the *other* way, it'll all be over; that'll be it for Queens.

"There was tremendous racial tension that summer. The riots started in Brooklyn as a result of neighborhood brawls between the blacks and the Italians. A retarded kid had been shot and killed by an unknown assailant and both sides decided to take it out on the cops.

"The rioting became so fierce that Mayor John Lindsay went out into the streets to try and mediate things. But they wouldn't listen. He was trapped somewhere, in a store, I think, and when he attempted to leave, they turned his car over and started setting fires. He had to scramble out and hide in an Italian restaurant. The cops couldn't even get in close enough to pull him out of there.

"There's been a lot of stories about what happened next— volumes of revisionist history, but I was there. I saw it.

"Somebody had the bright idea to run over to Joey Gallo's social club and see if he could calm things down enough for Lindsay to be rescued. At least he could talk some sense to the Italians. That was the plan.

"So Crazy Joey Gallo and John Lindsay had a sit-down. And Gallo took care of it for him. Just like two heads of state at a summit. The mob boss and the mayor.

"How Gallo did it, I don't know. But the word went out. Crazy Joe said to cool it. And to back it up, he put so many shooters out on the street that people got the idea. Now, Gallo had an ulterior motive. He was hoping that Lindsay would remember the favor. And who knows? Gallo probably saved John Lindsay's life.

"That became my first civics lesson as a policeman. What the cops couldn't accomplish, either a full-scale riot or organized crime could."

* * *

[9]

McCarthy had a friend, another rookie, whom they called the Shoe. All the Shoe ever wore were big, ugly, ripple-sole shoes. You could hear him coming before you saw him. Today, the Shoe is a captain in the Bronx.

"The Shoe was as strong as an ox. And just as shy. I never saw him go out with a girl. His marriage must have been arranged.

"We were in a skirmish line during the riots, like an old infantry formation, trying to move forward and clear one of the big avenues there. The Shoe is right beside me. All of a sudden, he gets tapped on the shoulder, and goes away with a woman from across the street.

"A little while later the Shoe crawls back to this kind of foxhole that we've set up behind an overturned car. The bastards are shooting at us again. We're pinned down like it's the D-day invasion—right in the middle of New York City. In a foxhole.

"The Shoe is ash-white, his face drained of any color. He looks like a ghost. His real name was Terry. I ask him, 'Terry, where have you been? We could've used you up here. These guys are shooting at us.'

"He stammers, 'I just delivered a baby.'

"'What?' Now, I know that the Shoe has never even seen a woman naked in his life. Never been to bed with anybody. The Shoe played baseball, that was it. I don't even think he knew where the hell babies came from. He was just like a big kid himself. And here he had to deliver a baby.

"'A baby.' He said it again. 'I did it. She told me what to do, this lady. It just popped out and I caught it—like I was playing second base.'"

The inexperienced cops from Bill McCarthy's rookie class who hit the streets in that summer of 1966 comprised the thinnest of blue lines. On their heads they wore World War II–era army helmets, steel pots, and in their hearts they carried the banners and all the working-class biases of places like Queens and Ozone Park and Bensonhurst.

The rookies were arranged in alphabetical order, by borough. The high command of the NYPD was bunkered in safety behind the paperwork walls of the old Police Headquarters at 240 Centre Street. They looked on as the riots of that summer meandered through some of the most dangerous real estate on earth, becoming one enormous brawl that spread from block to block and house to house.

Almost from the moment he put on the uniform, there was fighting all around McCarthy — behind, in front, on either side.

In one incident, a gentle kid named MacNamara manned the line with McCarthy. Suddenly, a single punch to the face knocked MacNamara down. McCarthy called for a medic — this was combat — but there were no medics. His friend just lay there bleeding. The only response that made any sense to McCarthy was to keep his head down and try and shield himself and MacNamara from the debris and projectiles that people — including women and little kids — were pouring down on the rookie cops from rooftops and windows.

Nobody ever seemed to be in charge; the riots had all the makings of a massacre — a bureaucratic massacre — and none of the top cops wanted to be around to pick up the tab for it. The kid cops with McCarthy were lucky if they could even find a sergeant.

Despite the mass confusion, the incessant sirens and the tireless waves of rioters who kept charging the police lines, McCarthy felt very much alone; more like a spectator than a participant in his own life. He certainly didn't feel like a real cop — a real cop would have known what to do.

Already, he was inventing a defense mechanism against the cycloning action and fear. With calmness and detachment, McCarthy was distancing the person from the uniform, the man from his mission. In the eventful years to come, as a Vice cop, he would use this studied disengagement that he had learned on the streets of Harlem to assess his own performance against the unbending standards he was setting for himself.

As soon as the riots temporarily ran their course—in full retreat most of the time, the cops *didn't* put them down— McCarthy was assigned to the old 3-2 precinct in Harlem, at 135th Street and Eighth Avenue. Radio Motor Car #565, sector 7. He was pulling the 6:00 P.M. to 2:00 A.M. shift with Tuesdays and Wednesdays off.

That might have qualified as the single most dangerous intersection in the entire United States during that smoldering hot spell of 1966. McCarthy would float as one of the extra bodies, dividing his time between the 3-2 in Harlem and the 7-3 or 7-9 in Brooklyn, where he had met Joey Gallo's crew.

His first official "day" at the 3-2 in Harlem was a sweltering Thursday night before the July Fourth weekend. Every cop in New York was expecting the worst.

He arrived for his first-ever roll call along with ten other rookies. There is nothing more fabled in the mind of the public than the ritual of police roll call. That included McCarthy himself. He expected to see what he had seen on television and in the movies—rows of crisply uniformed police officers thoughtfully logging that day's schedule as a caring, wise old sergeant looked on.

"Right in the middle of my first-ever roll call a black lady comes running in, wearing a raincoat, crying, in hysterics; and she goes up to the desk sergeant, screaming, 'The motherfucker did it, the motherfucker did it!' She opens her raincoat; she's naked and one of her breasts is cut off.

"She's bleeding, pulling her coat open so the desk sergeant can get a better look; she's cut up like something they just yanked up off the table from surgery—but this isn't surgery, this is where I'm supposed to go to work every day.

"I'm ready to pass out, but the old desk sergeant is bored stiff. He half raises himself up off his chair, and I can see him looking at the tit that's been cut off, kind of comparing it with the one that's still there. He yawns, just points to a bench over on the side and says to her, 'Shut the fuck up and sit the fuck down. We'll get to you.' And that was it.

"Then, one of the other rookies comes back with a guy who went nuts, wacko; tore his clothes off in a taxicab and he's screaming something about he's gonna lose his scholarship. And of course, nobody pays any attention *at all* to him because he isn't bleeding. They don't even bother to tell him to go sit in the corner. He just stands in the middle of the room raving.

"And I'm saying to myself, 'Do I really want to go out those doors?'

"That roll call turned out to set the pattern for all the rest— twenty-one years' worth.

"It was some old guy who hadn't been out from behind his desk in twenty years standing up there and droning on, reading the internal orders—and nobody in the place paying any attention to him—as he tried to tell *you*, who had just been under enemy fire, what the conditions were like out on the street. It was insanity.

"Other roll calls depended on which boss was working. Some of them were frustrated military types and the roll call sergeants had to keep them happy. That kind would actually inspect uniforms. The old guys really laughed at that. They'd make you go up and bend over, turn around and hold up the tails of your coat so they could see if you had a shine on your ass. And guys would always be trying to pass gas while they did it. That was twenty years ago. Now, if I told that to the kids today they would never believe it."

The plan called for one rookie each to be paired with one senior police officer; by breaking up the teams of veteran partners the police would be able to double the number of patrol cars on the street during the peak hours of the summer disturbances. There was only one problem: The older cops didn't want any part of the rookies.

* * *

"Seven of the nine rookies who went out before me, at six P.M., were back before six-forty-five P.M. with arrests — for gambling, narcotics, assault.

"The senior cops had all gone out and gotten rid of the rookies as fast as they could by giving them the first collar they saw. Anything to dump them. They didn't want them around while they were out doing their normal corrupt routine; doing their shakedowns, in other words. They couldn't trust us. And they certainly weren't about to split a note with a rookie.

"And this is all on the first night — in my first hour in Harlem. This is my real indoctrination into the NYPD.

"The person I was assigned to ride with happened to be over at a hospital with a psycho. So I was the last rookie to be picked up. I was standing there, waiting, like a little kid at the bus stop. I expected them to tell me to go sit next to the woman with the one tit.

"When I finally did get picked up, my partner's name was Mattie Morgan — Mad-Dog Morgan.

"I'll never forget him. He had a nightstick that looked like the leg of a piano. The thing was sculptured. He talked to it. He was a big, big guy, loud voice, like a wrestler.

"We're not out on patrol ten minutes and as soon as we pass the first liquor store in our sector, we hear gunshots.

"Three guys come running out of the liquor store and the next thing I know, we've got the three of them up against the wall. They're in handcuffs.

"I can't believe it. I'm numb. I still can't get the woman with her tit cut off out of my mind, but I've already seen a shootout and I'm making a felony arrest. Guns drawn.

"Just before we got them, one of the holdup men threw a .45 automatic down the stairs of a tenement. Mad-Dog hated cellars, he was afraid of rats, so he sent me down to get the gun.

"I go down these wooden stairs. They were not solid stairs, just like lattice steps, and there was all kinds of shit down there in the darkness, boxes, junk, old mattresses, there was even standing water in these deep smelly puddles; rats, too, I'm sure.

But I'm all gung ho, looking around for the gun.

"Damn, if I don't find a cocked .45 automatic. I was so delighted that I found it, that without even thinking, I pass it up, in the darkness, still cocked, through the stairs steps, to Morgan. I had it by the barrel with the barrel end facing me. If I had knocked it against the step, I would have shot myself.

"We go back to the station house; Morgan's got his chance to get rid of me. So I'm gonna take the collar.

"'Kid,' he says, 'you got the collar. Good man. You'll probably get a day off for this.'

"Meanwhile, he's gonna kiss off, get back his own partner and go out and do whatever they want to do.

"At the station house there's already nine collars ahead of me, all rookies. Now, these old guys didn't make nine collars in a month. But the captain in the precinct doesn't want to lose the best arrest statistics he's had since he's been there. He comes out of his office and says, 'Uh uh, the rookies ain't takin' no collars. Only senior men.'

"Since we weren't real cops at that point the credit for our arrests would not have gone to his precinct but would have reverted back to the academy. Naturally, this change in their plans really pissed off the senior cops because now they were stuck with all the paperwork. And they were still stuck with us. I think that captain damn near had a mutiny right there.

"That was my first patrol. And I couldn't get over it— fifteen minutes and a quarter; that's all it took to go to Harlem. Four or five people were shot that night, all kinds of armed robberies, people screaming. And this was the *calm* between the fights."

The old-timers were out to break in the rookies—and break them in fast. Dirty tricks were commonplace. They would send the young cops into a tenement, sometimes to serve a warrant, often just to teach them a lesson. "Come on over here, kid. We need you, kid." That's how it always started. The old cops would knock on a tenement door, practically bash it in, pretend that an arrest was about to be made, and then, as soon as the door began to creak open an inch, shove the rookies in front of it and run like hell.

It was frightening for the people inside the apartment, humiliating for the rookies, disastrous for already tense police community relations, but the warped old cops considered it great sport.

"One of these old cops was a thief, a crooked, big, fat slob; he must have weighed about 260 pounds. I gave away about a hundred pounds to him, maybe more. I was skinny then. He convinced all the rookies that he was some kind of hero. He was like the Pied Piper. All the new cops followed him, tried to imitate him.

"One day I found out that he gave a traffic summons for illegal parking to a cop, just to be a prick—that was a huge joke to him. But this particular cop was parked over by a cancer hospital because he had his little kid in there. He was getting chemotherapy. He comes out of the hospital and finds out that his car has been towed away. I happened to be in the precinct when the poor guy came in. As a matter of fact, I lent him the money to pay to get his car out of the impound lot.

"And there's this big slob laughing his ass off, over behind the sergeant's desk, because he had really screwed this man with the sick child. I got him out of there in a hurry because I didn't want him to have to get in a fight, too. And I just waited.

"At the end of the day I went up to the slob in the locker room and said. 'Why'd you give that guy a ticket over at the cancer hospital?' And he lied. He denied that he was the one who did it. But I had seen the summons with his signature on it. I called him a liar to his face.

"We were changing our clothes, ready to go off-duty. But I didn't care. This was worth it. I took off after that animal and I chased him down Twelfth Avenue in my shorts. And I'm proud to say that when I caught up with him I gave him an old-fashioned ass kicking. And we were in the same squad. We worked the same jobs. After that, he would never let himself be in the locker room at the same time that I was there."

The worst precinct in the city at that time was the 7-9, in Bedford Stuyvesant, on Gates Avenue. The police station had been put under siege more than once by the neighborhood, and usually, the only cops who were assigned there were the kind who had made powerful enemies—or the rookies like McCarthy.

"This one hot, rainy night I was working with a black officer. The guy had muscles. His shirt was pulled tight across his chest and arms like a weight lifter. His head was shaved bald and he had medals that ran up his shoulder and down his back. He had so many medals he looked like a Mexican general.

"I get in the car with him, and the very first thing he says to me is, 'They teaching you any of that civil rights bullshit at the police academy?'

"I said, 'All the time.' What else was I supposed to say?

"'We got some mighty fine caves over here,' he said.

"I'm thinking—*Caves? What's he talking about?*

"The first thing he does is pull the car off the street so we can go into an after-hours club. There's only one white guy in the bar—me. They pour my partner a shot of whiskey, about six ounces straight, no ice. He polishes that off and then he hands me a glass too. I just held it and looked at it. Then, the girls come up and start to feel his muscles. We're saved by the radio.

"We get a call—'Psycho in the cellar.' That's a crazy person who's in the basement of a tenement. You could get ten calls like that a night.

"We go to this house, down to the basement and there's nobody there. Then he says, 'Ain't this a mighty fine cave, boy? The caves is where the animals live.' Now I know.

"The person who had made this call lived up in a fourth-floor walkup. We go up there, me and this real cop. I'm right behind him.

"We pass a woman in the hallway. She's smiling at me, and she's walking as if she's headed out of the building. About thirty years old, black. I was very concerned about modesty and it was a very narrow hallway, so I pressed myself up against the wall to avoid bumping into her breasts. My face was turned the other way to allow her to pass by and give her the most room.

"The real cop now starts to look back for me and he sees that the woman has a knife at her side. But I don't notice a thing. She's the psycho in the cellar we were supposed to get. She's still smiling, very strangely, and she comes right up to me. I have no idea what's going on.

"All of a sudden, she lunges at me with the knife, and I go down. My partner has already reacted—he jumped on her and caught the sleeve of her blouse, but didn't get her arm fast enough. She sticks me in the side, in the love handle on the left. I never even saw it coming.

"I wasn't hurt very badly; we had to get the cuffs on her before she tried anything else.

"I get one handcuff around her wrist; she's holding the other handcuff in her free hand and she's fighting, and I'm still trying to subdue her without touching her breast.

"My partner is behind her and I'm in front. She kicks me in the balls about three times, and the real cop is actually *letting* her kick me. He wants this to be a lesson.

"We finally get her handcuffed, and my partner goes upstairs to get the complainant, who was this woman's aunt. He leaves me downstairs, he's so disgusted with me. 'Can you take care of her now?' he asks.

"I have her up against the wall, handcuffed, but damn, she keeps coming at me. I'm still too bashful to touch her tits and this just isn't working. I get nailed in the balls again. Hard.

"The real cop can't take any more. He comes flying down from the fourth-floor landing and just jumps on her.

"He bangs her right off the wall. That's it. I honest-to-God thought he put her right into the next apartment—I could see plaster dust; I thought he stuck her through the wall.

"After all that, after we finally got that psycho bitch under control, we went back to the station house. I could either arrest her or "psycho" her. Just take her to Bellevue. You don't need a supervisor for that. So there's less paperwork involved.

"Now, I'm bleeding a little bit from the stab wound. So the black cop says to me, 'Do you want to go sick? You gotta go see the surgeon. He'll come to your house.'

"I said, 'Whatta you mean, he'll come to my house?'

"'Yeah, the next day, if you go sick, the sergeant on patrol will make sure you don't go out of the house.'

"'You mean my mother will find out? I can't let my mother know. She never wanted me to be a cop.'

"He says, 'Sure, the guy will come to your house to make sure you aren't faking.'

"I didn't want to go sick after I heard that. I was afraid that if my mother ever found out that I'd already gotten hurt, that would be the end of my police career. So we psycho-warded the woman with the knife. They all liked me after that because I had just saved them a ton of paperwork—on the arrest and on my going sick.

"The riots taught me that I had to ambush people. I didn't give them a chance. I mugged them. Dance contests go on. Fights don't. Fifteen seconds and the fight's over. I'm not a headhunter. If you know what you're doing, go for the body. If you want to win a street fight, that's how you do it. They never expect that.

"People think that cops know how to fight. They don't. They're scared. Like everybody else. Like I was scared—all the time. You don't learn how to take a punch going to the police academy for twelve weeks.

"After that episode in Harlem my whole approach to the bad guys changed. It became what I call the *rodeo method*. It was like roping a steer. Get him cuffed, get him down, get him under control. Then he can't hurt you and the show's over. As I gained experience, I rarely hit anybody because hitting never got anybody handcuffed."

[19]

THREE

You *are* a *Cop* for life, just like a priest. If somebody
had told me then that I would spend the rest of my life
as a cop I would have laughed in their face. Or maybe
spit in it.

MOTHER'S MAXIM

HELL'S KITCHEN, 1945

Bill McCarthy was born hopelessly Irish and incorrigibly Catholic on March 6, 1945, at Saint Claire's Hospital in Hell's Kitchen, on the West Side. Today, it's an AIDS hospice.

His family lived in Jackson Heights, Queens, in a house on Ninety-second Street. He was the third of five children, with two older, mothering sisters and a younger brother and sister. Their grandmother lived with them. She spoke Gaelic and had gone to the sixth book in Ireland, a remarkable educational achievement for a woman of her generation. She knew a thousand poems; a poem for any occasion.

His father was a supervisor in a foundry—the Neptune Meter Company—in Long Island City. He'd started out as a molder and would spend the next thirty-one years feeling the furnace blast—never less than 135 or 140 degrees.

"The earliest memory I have is jumping off the stoop of our church on a Sunday afternoon and landing on a broken bottle and the glass puncturing my wrist and my blood running all over the place. My father put his hand over my wrist and ran everywhere in the neighborhood, trying to find a doctor's office that was open. And when he finally did get a doctor, he couldn't take his hand off my wrist because my blood had coagulated on him; his hand had frozen solid. I still have the scar—it was just one sixteenth of an inch from hitting the vein you want when you try to commit suicide.

"My father is about five feet six, 165 pounds, a small, brick-hard Irishman, but he had a size fourteen ring—he had hands that were like a shoemaker's hands. Hard as sandpaper.

"In the foundry where he worked, you took these sand molds that weighed between 110 and 115 pounds and you poured melted brass or steel to make a utility meter, and he would pick up that form and put it on a conveyor belt. My father would pick up about 150 pounds two or three hundred times a day.

"They used to supply the foundrymen with beer in buckets and salt tablets. If you didn't drink the beer you dropped dead. They would stay in there ten or twelve hours a day. Summer and winter.

"My father was totally responsible. For him, very simply, that meant he worked very hard, brought his check home and gave it to my mother. Entertainment was Lawrence Welk on a Saturday night. Throughout my childhood, we said the family rosary every night at seven o'clock. My father was disciplined. He ate the same lunch for thirty-one years—ham and cheese on day-old Wonder bread, rye, and on Fridays, it was American cheese with mustard.

"He gave up drinking as a sacrifice to God when my mother was pregnant with my youngest sister, Madeline. They were both supposed to die, the baby was so premature. They didn't and he always said that the only reason was because he made that vow. He never touched liquor again in his life. He believed that he had cut a deal with God and he had to stick to it. It's been thirty-seven years now and he still hasn't had a drink.

"My mother died very young of a blood clot that lodged in her lung. I was there in the hospital with my father; I was a cop then. He turned to me, looked into my eyes and said, 'She's not dead, only asleep, because she's still warm.'

"He had already given up cake for my Uncle Tommy to go on the wagon, and that had worked. He stayed sober for ten years. And he truly believed that he had saved Madeline and my mother once. But this time, God hadn't let him know in time, so there was nothing left that he could give up. My father was a strong-willed man.

"I had to pronounce my mother dead to my father. 'She's not alive, she's not breathing, there's no pulse. Look!'

"Then, he turned to me with these big, awful tears in his eyes and said, 'If He only let me know; what could I have given up?'"

McCarthy had been a ferocious, dedicated schoolyard basketball player. One hectic summer he actually wore out two basketballs traveling all over the city scuffling to get into the best games, like the schoolyard classics at 108th Street in Rockaway where the spectacular Maguire brothers took on all comers. They were do-or-die shootouts.

To play at 108th Street you had to win. If you lost, you didn't get to play the rest of the day because there were twenty teams stacked up behind you waiting for their chance. In that era Rockaway was the best pressure basketball in New York, and McCarthy managed to stay on good teams and play all day long. And he didn't do it on talent, he did it on persistence, on endurance.

Nobody practiced longer or harder. He developed incredible stamina, taught himself to be relentless, especially on in-your-face defense, never letting up. He agitated and annoyed and almost always found some way to beat you.

"After grade school, Blessed Sacrament Grammar School in Jackson Heights, I went to Power Memorial at Sixty-first Street and Tenth Avenue. The Irish Christian Brothers. I was there with Lew Alcindor, with Kareem. I was a little ahead of him.

"I grew up boxing. I boxed every Friday night of my life. I boxed the way most kids play basketball. I can't do it anymore. I'm too old and my timing's shot. But I loved it; couldn't get enough of punching that heavy bag.

"I practiced boxing in a club, had a gym in my basement. My father was a boxer. A man who dated a girl in my building was a professional boxer. I learned how to box. I got into the Joe Louis thing when I was fourteen years old.

"I wrestled for one year when I was in college. I always lifted weights. Then later, in the police department, I sparred nine rounds every week.

"Now, if you're familiar with being hit, you can assess if it's actually a good punch or not. Your response is based more upon the physical reality of the punch as opposed to the social, psychic surprise.

"I might have thought, Oh, he didn't hit that hard. That wasn't a good punch. His technique is terrible. I've made an assessment. I'm not in shock. I had that advantage over every other cop I knew.

"That's why most white people can't take a punch—not even white prizefighters. If they get knocked out, they get knocked out from *shock*, not from the power of the punch. They may never have been hit before, not really hit. Black people get hit all the time. There's a difference.

"As a learning tool, you really cannot overestimate the value of being knocked on your ass.

"I've been knocked out three times, but never on the job. I've also been hit on the head with a pipe. I've been kicked in the head. A guy tried to steal my basketball in the park when I was seventeen years old, and two other guys jumped me and beat me until I was unconscious. I crawled under a car and just lay there.

"I was also stabbed when I was in high school.

"I was on a staircase in a public school during the race riots and I just happened to be in their way—six black girls. They stuck an umbrella right through me, underneath my belt. Just stuck it in me and then they were trying to beat the shit out of me when another guy came down the staircase. I was on my way up to play basketball on the fourth floor. Oh, man, did that hurt!

"I had my jaw broken in college. A sucker punch. I didn't get knocked out. The guy broke the bone that connected the jaw to the skull. It wasn't shattered, just knocked off the hook.

"I was at Saint Francis College in Loretto, Pennsylvania, outside Pittsburgh. There was a seminary there and I was thinking of "going up the hill," as they called it. That meant going into the seminary to study for the priesthood. It just so happened that in Loretto the seminary was separate from the rest of the college, way up on top of one of the Allegheny Mountains. That's where the expression came from—to go up the hill. This was before Millie, before the police department.

"It was Ash Wednesday. I came back from 6:00 o'clock mass to the dormitory, and I said, 'Lent, Lent, Lent! No women, no women, no women!' And I took his girlfriend's picture, folded it up politely, and put it in the garbage pail. That was enough to set this guy off. He's a disc jockey in Pittsburgh now—at least he used to be."

Like every first-born male in a traditional Irish Catholic family, McCarthy's soul, as well as his ass, should have belonged to the church. Without so much as a word of consultation with him, his mother had preordained him for the priesthood, for bishop or better.

She promised him that he if did take his vows, she would have her engagement ring melted down so that she could put the diamonds in his first chalice. That way, every time he consecrated the host he could think of her. At the very least, she instilled in her son a very noisy conscience.

"'Be a good man'—that's what my mother used to whisper in my ear. I was dedicated to being a good person. To saving my immortal soul, to gaining my rightful place in heaven. To her, that was an end in itself. Scrupulosity, that was me. I have never missed communion on Sunday in my life but twice. I had pneu-

[24]

monia, I think. I have never missed mass, never just rolled over in bed on a Sunday morning. I can't. She wouldn't let me— alive or dead. I did become an altar boy and that appeased her somewhat. But I knew that I'd let her down."

When he married the former Milagros Concepcion Rodriguez-Medina on September 17, 1967, McCarthy's life quickly refocused itself. That event, probably more than anything else, made him decide to become a cop. But, as he told himself, he would only stay on as a short-timer; he was just in it for the paycheck.

"Becoming a cop was, for me at least, the psychological equivalent of going into the Peace Corps. That's how it was in the 1960s.

"It was only years later that I realized a policeman's life was right for me. The combination of energy, enthusiasm, honesty, and violence—I had to find something that could accommodate all those things.

"As I went along in school I was greatly affected by the concept of the 'guardians' in Plato. I believed that I was destined to be a guardian, a protector.

"They needed cops back then. You could walk in there on a Saturday morning without an appointment and take the exam. A friend of mine was going to take the police test and he says to me, 'You wanna take the test?' I figured, why not.

"On a Saturday morning in November 1965, I walked in and took it. I think I got a ninety-seven. And then I forgot all about it.

"About six months later, when I was a sophomore in college, I get a letter from the City of New York. It begins, 'You will be appointed June 20th....'

"*Appointed! Holy Shit!* I didn't know what I'd gotten myself into. But then, I sat down and figured, I *will* need a summer job. I was gonna do push-ups at the police academy, I was gonna

[25]

get paid for doing push-ups and I was gonna quit in September. It was a goof. I was a jock, I was going to go to boot camp for the summer, work out, build up the pecs.

"I had a part-time job in a bank that summer, and my last week there I see this knock-out girl coming in as a teller-trainee. Her name was Millie. She was Puerto Rican. All of a sudden that didn't make one damn bit of difference.

"I went right up to her and said, 'So, when are we going out for dinner?' But she didn't want any part of me. She was very sophisticated, especially compared to me, and at the time, she was living on her own in Manhattan and was going out with a guy who owned two nightclubs. Millie was a high society person as far as I was concerned. I used to wear Bermuda shorts, torn shirts, and I rode this little motor scooter.

"I got her address from work and I went up to this house and I rang the bell. 'Is Millie here?'

"A woman opened the window on the second floor and screamed something in Spanish, then, 'She not here.' I started to give her a real hard time. I'm the only white guy there. Then, I realize that I have the wrong address. Millie had moved and they never made the change at work. And I see all these Puerto Rican men starting to close in on me. And right there on the spot, I figured out how to apologize in Spanish.

"A couple days later, I found the right place. 'I'm here to have dinner,' I told her, but immediately, I can see that it isn't working.

"'You have some nerve just coming in here.' She was mad.

"'Okay. You still have to eat. I'll take you out.'

"She went into the bedroom to change her clothes. I followed her in and sat on the bed. That was the wrong move.

"She became outraged, started screaming. I had stepped over the line. I had violated the law that said a nice girl does not invite strange guys into her bedroom. And believe me, I was strange then.

"But I calmed her down. We did go out to dinner. And we got married. It all happened so quickly. I was all set to make some fast money as a cop, but only temporarily; squeeze every drop I could out of the job, save up, get a handyman's special out in Levittown and start banging out the little rabbits.

"Let me tell you that twenty years ago, to walk into an Irish house in Queens with a Puerto Rican girl and say you're going to drop out of college and become a cop in order to marry her—that was an event.

"And it didn't bother me that everybody in Millie's family were cop-haters. Including Millie. But I was a cop before she tried to talk me out of it, before she even met me. My wife hated the police. She was afraid of them. She grew up on the other side. If a cop came to the door, she wouldn't answer it. Not even today.

"When she was a little girl the cops had come into her neighborhood for some reason, run into her uncle or some relative; there was a fight and the cops killed him right there on the street. Shot him in the head, right in front of the kids. They were the kind of cops I worked with as a rookie.

"I stayed Irish and she stayed Puerto Rican. My marriage was the ultimate melting pot. The kids we produced were cultural by-products. It was like cooking my corned beef with garlic. I'll never forget what happened the day that our daughter Christine was christened. Both of our families had gotten together at the church, for the ceremony, and everything had gone well there. They were perfectly civil to each other.

"Later, during the party I was talking and drinking and feeling pretty good, and decided to check on the baby. Then, all of a sudden, I couldn't see the baby anywhere. Millie was busy, too—but Christine wasn't with her, either.

"I got a little nervous. Was the baby sick? Where was she? So I went looking through the apartment to see who had her. I found her in her crib in one of the bedrooms.

"I'll never forget what I saw. There she was—all in white, like a tiny doll—she was sound asleep. Smiling. It looked like Millie's relatives had raided their local botanica and had put all the stuff on Christine's crib. And there was an old woman in that bedroom; she was standing very close to the crib, chanting. There was a little sack of black cowhide, curled like a monkey's paw. It was hanging around Christine's little pink neck.

"I told Millie later on that she better not expect to see any of that at the Irish Catholic christenings that my sisters had.

"I guess I didn't marry an Irish girl because that would have been like marrying an echo—one, holy, Catholic, and apostolic.

"There always seemed to me to be something magic about Latin girls. They'd say, 'I wonder what they're giving at the movies?' instead of, 'I wonder what's at the movies?' I thought that was the sexiest thing I'd ever heard.

"Marrying a policeman or becoming involved with a policeman was not the sort of thing for a Puerto Rican person to do. A policeman was the enemy, whether you did anything wrong or not.

"In the summer, on a hot night, when they put on the fire hydrants for the kids to cool off, Millie and her little brother used to go under the water.

"One night they didn't hear the other kids yell 'la hara,' which was the signal that the cops were coming. They got caught and the cops put them—these two little kids—in the back of a police car and just rode around the block. Then they brought them back, showed everybody that they meant business, and turned off the fire hydrant.

"That was the day that Millie learned to hate the cops."

FOUR

A *Station House* is a cop's ghetto. It's dirty, filthy green, it's beat-up old lockers and showers that don't work and toilets with no doors on the stalls or paper on the rolls. It's home.

M O T H E R ' S   M A X I M

■

B R O W N S V I L L E ,   1 9 6 6

A sniper had barricaded himself on an apartment rooftop. His real target had been a police sergeant who was leading a riot patrol on the street below. But the sniper's aim was faulty and he had killed a child instead.

McCarthy was one of the cops in that patrol. He heard the gunfire, but had no idea where it had come from. Then he saw a child who was playing on the pavement across the street suddenly go down, blood geysering from a huge hole in his small chest.

As he and the other cops started running across the street to try to help the little boy who had been shot, more projectiles—rocks, bottles, chunks of concrete—rained down on them in the murky silence of the humid night. Suddenly, the men on either side of McCarthy dropped down to avoid the debris. Pinned down, the patrol had to sit it out until reinforcements finally pulled them to safety.

* * *

[29]

"I remember another big, big, *huge* retarded kid. I was walking down the block and this woman comes up to me and tells me her son won't go into the house; he has to go in for dinner. I check him out and he has to be at least 350 pounds. Just a brute of a kid.

"She's screaming, 'Officer, officer, my son won't come into the house. Will you help me get him into the house?' And I went over to that guy. He could've eaten me, could've swallowed me whole. I talked to him for a while and guess what? I ended up in total agreement with him. If he didn't want to go back into that house that was fine with me. You know why? Because I was the only one there who was about to *make* him go back inside and I didn't really care what he did as long as he didn't eat me. That single incident was a valuable part of my education as a cop—knowing when to make a stand and when to look the other way.

"There are plenty of times when the best, most ethical, most moral decision a cop can make is to look the other way. This was one of those times. The situation did not call for me trying to fight this big kid. For what? For his mother to feel like she was still his boss? That whole neighborhood was just waiting for me to use a stick or a jack on that kid, waiting for some excuse to hate me. I refused to give it to them."

Later that summer, McCarthy was an extra man again. The police were so short of bodies that they were assigning rookies to work with other rookies. None of them had a clue as to what they were supposed to be doing.

It was here that McCarthy really came to appreciate the infantry aspect of police work. Even patrol cars were scarce; in those days they used to let the rookies off at a certain corner and return eight hours later to pick them up again—provided, of course, that they had survived their tour.

"Cops who become too dependent on their guns act that way because they have never learned how to be *alone* on the street.

"Now, when a guy comes into the job, he instantly gets a partner, he gets training. He never works alone. He never has to learn how to talk to people. He can spend his entire tour talking to his partner, never talking to a citizen, and when they do have to talk to citizens, they don't know how. They're rude, crude, and abrupt.

"In 1966, you only got back to the station house alive if you knew how to be a diplomat. You had to be Henry Kissinger. It was all ingenuity and resourcefulness. You had to cajole, and encourage, and get them to cooperate with you if you were alone. There were no radios, phones, not that many police cars.

"It was very lonely if you didn't talk to the people.

"When I started a late tour alone, if I saw a bum on the street, that bum did the late tour with me. I wouldn't let him go. If a drunk or wino walked by me, I made him stay with me. I'd talk with a wino the whole night. I'd stand in a doorway with that guy, I'd even get him cigarettes, I'd buy him coffee, and I'd talk to him—ask him what's the story, where's he from, why is he here and I'd just get to know him and that would make the night pass by.

" 'You're under arrest. Your job is to keep me company.' That was my line on the late shift.

"People on the street are much younger than they appear. People who look sixty years old could be twenty nine. Incredible people, bright people, very accomplished people, who, all of a sudden, had the plug come out of the wall and they fall apart.

"Most of the policemen I knew, in Vice especially, did not respect themselves or other people. I made a promise to myself in the very beginning that I would never let that happen to me."

Regardless of their good intentions, however, it was almost impossible for rookies like McCarthy not to surrender to the hardening cynicism of the job. His own turn came when he and his partner, another rookie, were out on patrol when they spotted a blazing fire erupting from the upper stories of a tenement.

"About three blocks ahead of us I looked up and saw this smoke pouring out of a building. Now, being the track star, I tell the other guy, 'Go find a fire alarm and pull the box.'

"I sprint the three blocks and there are about forty or fifty black people across the street; as I get there, I scream, 'Is there anybody in the building?' The crowd starts saying, 'Two old ladies on the third floor; two old ladies on the third floor. Two old ladies on the third floor.' They're chanting.

"So I go into the building. The place is in flames; thick, thick smoke, it was like breathing dirt. And I get up to the second-floor landing and part of the wall collapsed, the floor collapsed. It was black and filthy, and I was choking and I can still hear them chanting: 'Two old ladies on the third floor, two old ladies on the third floor.' And I was embarrassed. I was afraid to come out without the two old ladies.

"There was an exposed waste pipe on the wall, so I tried to shimmy up the waste pipe, thinking I'm going to get their attention by banging my nightstick on the wall. I took a couple more deep gasps of breath and started banging. But then, I must have blacked out because I fell off the waste pipe, hit my head on the landing, and somehow, I ended up down on the first floor. The floorboards must have given way and I just dropped like a rock.

"When I came to, a couple firemen were pulling me out into the street; I was vomiting, choking, and heaving. My uniform was smoldering.

"I remember being taken to the hospital and there were all these people with green outfits on, green masks, and they were putting this oxygen thing on my face. I'm coughing, I couldn't stop coughing; I couldn't breathe. Then, this person in a surgical gown—I don't know if it was a man or woman—was coming at me with this needle that looked about four feet long; they were coming right at my face with this needle. I thought, Jesus Christ, it's gonna go right through the bed. But they stuck it through my mask instead of through me. I was still hacking my lungs out, saying, Jesus, thank God they didn't put that in me.'

"Several hours later, I'm still hacking and the sergeant on patrol walks into my hospital room and asks, 'Are you going sick, kid?'

"'Should I go sick?'

"He says, 'Listen, that's up to you. Do you wanta go sick or not?'

"I said, 'Is the guy still gonna come to my house?'

"'Yeah,' he answers.

"'Never mind,' I told him. My mother couldn't find out about this, either.

"'Fine,' he says, and takes me back to the station house. My uniform smells of smoke. They're practically dragging me up the steps, but there's no way I can go sick. Everybody's glad again—no paperwork for them.

"There was an old Irish lieutenant on the desk wearing these thick, Coke-bottle glasses. He doesn't even look up. I'm coughing my lungs out.

"'What the hell is the matter with you?' he asks. 'Do you think you're a fucking fireman?' And still, he hasn't even looked at me.

"I almost started to cry. I'm saying to myself—here I run three blocks, I go into the building to try and save two old ladies, I fall, black out, maybe almost get killed and what do I get? This jerk is giving me a hard time.

"So now I go in the back room and my partner's there. I haven't seen him since the fire, since I sent him to yank the call box. I say, 'Jesus Christ, what are we supposed to do? We're cops, aren't we supposed to go in after people in a burning building?'

"He just looks at me in this funny way, like he knows something he's not supposed to know and says, 'They're angry with you because nobody has lived in that building for the last six months. The crowd lied to us. We fell for it. They just wanted to get us killed. The old guys told me they do it all the time around here, any time a white cop's involved.' And then he looked at the floor like his heart was about to break and walked away from me."

[33]

FIVE

There are two *Penal Laws,* two books; a big one and a
little one. The normal civilian wants you to deal with
him by the little book, but for the rest of the world they
want you to smack it in the head with the big book.

MOTHER'S MAXIM

■

MANHATTAN

"When I finally got out of Harlem, I had a chance to make the
first arrest that really taught me how the justice system worked.

"I was on Madison Avenue in Manhattan and I heard a
woman scream. I saw a guy jump out of a Volkswagen, knock
her down and steal her purse. I was a rookie and I was with
two old-timers. I was yelling at them when I saw the guy jump
back in the car. I wanted to chase the guy, but they didn't want
to be bothered. 'What's the hurry, kid?'

"They said, 'Are you gonna take the collar?' In other words
they didn't want to make an arrest or have to go to court. 'Are
you gonna take the collar, kid? You want it or don't you?'

"I said, 'Yeah, I'll take the collar.'

"So the car went up a couple more blocks: Madison Avenue
is northbound and they turned down to go east on some street
off of Madison; they crossed Park, made a right turn, now going
southbound on Lexington. Then we get stuck in traffic on the
eastbound side.

"I jumped out of the car on Park Avenue and ran east to
Lexington. When I turned onto Lexington Avenue, there was

the Volkswagen, almost angle-parked in a bus stop with the engine running and the doors open. But the car was empty. There I am, empty car, doors open and there's nobody around.

"I happened to look into a shoe store, and there was a guy with combat boots on, sitting on the shoe stand, like he was going to get a shoe shine, except his chest was heaving. So I ran in and grabbed him and dragged him out of the store, tore him off the seat. I just knew it was the right guy. I never saw him, but some guy with combat boots on isn't getting a shine. He was a beat-up guy with an army jacket on. A young guy in his twenties.

"As I was dragging him outside, there was another man coming out of a candy store and he just had this surprised look on his face, so I grabbed him, too.

"Then I dragged them both back and finally, the radio patrol car came—the two old-timers had been chasing them sort of casually—I threw them into the car and we went back to the lady. She said they were the guys, all right.

"Now, in the car there were eleven pocketbooks. The car was stolen. There were eleven different pocketbooks from eleven different street robberies, in addition to the twelfth pocketbook of this lady.

"So when I went to court, I had thirteen complainants—the owner of the car and the owners of the twelve pocketbooks. All of the complainants, by the third court appearance, were pissed at me because all they wanted were their pocketbooks and the car back, all of which were evidence; but I was the hump who wouldn't give them back their pocketbooks.

"The two thieves were very different. The rich kid had a private attorney; the poor kid had a public defender. They were going to make a plea bargain. The rich kid was going to get a suspended sentence; his mother was in publishing. And the poor kid—his father was a nonunion plumber or something—he was going to have to do time. That was my first taste of 'justice.' And that was also the first time I really learned what the public thinks of the police.

"The public wants to be safe. They want to be able to go to

the store without getting mugged and when they go back home they want to find their television still in their living room. And they don't ever want to see your face, otherwise. Don't interfere with them. Don't give them a traffic ticket. Don't get in their way because you are the hired help."

In February 1967, over nine months after the riots, they finally sent McCarthy's class to the police academy on Twentieth Street in Manhattan, on the East Side, between Second and Third avenues.

At that time the course of instruction was supposed to last four months, with one major test scheduled following each month. Fail one test and you were automatically washed out. At least that's what the curriculum called for. With McCarthy's class, however—already wounded, bloodied street cops—some exceptions had to be made.

"I only took two tests, spent a grand total of two weeks there and graduated. They needed us back on the street again.

"By then, after the riots, in the summer of 1966, after some of the action we had seen, a few of our guys already had medals and most of us looked like we had *ninety-mission hats*. That's one of the odd quirks in the NYPD—at least it was then. You could tell what kind of a cop a man was by the way he wore his uniform hat. With rookies and deskmen the hard visor would be shiny and the peak stiff; the more time you spent on the street, the more battered the hat became. The really *bad* guys—and by then we were the baddest of the bad, or at least we thought we were—would take the stiffening out of the round part of the hat, smash down the peak and fold it up and wear the hat with the sides pegged back like the old World War II flying aces, hence the name: a mission hat. Like you had flown ninety missions or something and lived to tell about it. Now, a cop had to *earn* the right to wear a mission hat. You could not fake that. The other cops would *know*.

[36]

"Each individual cop runs the police department. I learned that early. The political clique at the top do what they want to do. They issue orders like crazy. But it's up to each individual cop how much actual service he's willing to give to people.

"Up until I left the academy for good, I had never been anywhere except an 'A' house. There's 'A,' 'B,' and 'C' houses. A 'C' house is very quiet. Maybe somewhere in Queens, no real crimes. A 'B' is a little busier, not much. An 'A' house is the highest enforcement activity, the most undesirable, as far as safety. And all of my precincts were 'A' houses during the riots—the 3-2, the 7-3, the 7-9. There's very little difference anymore. They're all bad. If you want to get a preferred assignment later on, as part of your career path, you can accelerate the movement if you have had your dance card punched at an 'A' house.

"I assumed that when my probation was up I was just going to be assigned permanently to the 3-2 precinct, an 'A' house, because I already had a seat in a radio car there. I was like a regular. But technically, as a rookie, my permanent 'command' was still the police academy. My paycheck used to go to the police academy.

"At the end of my probation period, on our graduation day, in fact, in March 1967, I was sent downtown to pick up my own paycheck. Every two weeks they used to let one guy go down and pick up the paychecks for everybody. But for some reason, it was different this time. And we were suspicious.

"As soon as you stepped off the elevator at headquarters, they had people there directing you: If you speak Italian or Spanish, go over to this table. If you have a chauffeur's license or if you drive a truck, you go over to that table.

"I had a chauffeur's license to drive commercially. I used to drive a cab. And I used to drive a truck on the beach. I worked at the Surf Club in Rockaway; I used to drive a truck to pick up the garbage on the beach.

"So now I go back and two weeks later, the orders come out and I get assigned to the SOD—the Special Operations Division—Traffic, 'B.' They didn't even have their own tow truck squad then, but they wanted to start one with fifty six rookies. We had to use old sanitation department wreckers.

"The next thing I know I'm pulling traffic duty in downtown Manhattan and handing out summonses. Two months later, they start this tow squad and I was given one of the trucks. They never asked me—you're here, that's it. Drive.

"Traffic had been manned by dump jobs from all over the city. They didn't ask them. They forced them there. Like old-timers who were from shit-holes—shit-holes are places where you would do anything to get out but you were dumped there by commanders. Now, you had fifty six guys with eighteen, twenty years on the job—retreads, wrung-overs, dropouts, rejects, and then, all at once, you assign them there together with fifty six rookies.

"I got lucky. I'm only there a few months when they would occasionally take me off the tow truck and give me an assignment driving for one of the bosses. Eventually, I became the steady chauffeur for one particular sergeant—who is now my son's godfather.

"I chauffeured him around in a patrol car. A sergeant in those days was a big deal. They could even issue search warrants. They could do whatever they wanted to you and there was nothing you could do about it. There was no bill of rights for cops, no union lawyers or grievance committees.

"I discovered that this sergeant loved to get involved. He would actually make arrests, go in on other guys' busts if he could be of help; he acted like a leader. That was my very first experience with a boss who wasn't afraid to act like a real cop. He was the sergeant of all the sergeants that were up there. He'd roll on anything. The more problematic, the better. Racing along sidewalks, upstairs, fights, lock 'em up. This was an old-time, smash-'em-in-the-head-and-lock-'em-up sergeant. I loved it.

"There was no penalty for him to do all that because that man could type 120 words a minute. He could take a blank piece of paper and put it in the typewriter and type a finished report like a machine gun—all black, Underwood, perfect copy, first time out. Anything you wanted. That's the penalty of being involved. Paperwork. It has to be on paper."

The captain running the Traffic detail then was Kenneth Gussman. McCarthy had attracted his attention from the very beginning. Eventually, Gussman became McCarthy's "hook," his "rabbi," and was ultimately responsible for getting him into Vice. Anyone who intended to go places in the NYPD needed just such a hook to pull him along and yank him out of tight places. In their first meeting, however, Gussman didn't know what to make of this hip-shooting kid from Queens.

"I called Gussman a crook. That could have been a big mistake. I was in Traffic, Gussman's chauffeur, another tit-job. He gave me a dollar and told me to go buy him cigarettes.

"'I don't buy cigarettes for anybody. Get it yourself.'

"He said, 'What?'

"'No, get your own. I don't buy nobody cancer.'

"Later that night, I was eating a sandwich in the police station and he said, 'You're a pretty spunky kid. You don't talk to a police captain like that.'

"I just told him, not trying to be cocky at all, 'I don't buy anybody cancer. That's not my job description.' Then, we got talking. He tells me he used to work in the Sixth Division—that's the plainclothes division in Harlem.

"I said, 'Oh, you're a crook then.'

Gussman just looked at me.

"'Listen, if you were in the Sixth Division, in plainclothes, you were on the pad, because if you weren't on the pad they would have written a book about you and I wouldn't have had to be introduced to you when I met you. You would be a folk hero.' Gussman spent the rest of that night trying to convince me that he wasn't corrupt. Finally, he tells me that he's going to keep his eye on me. We never talked about it again."

* * *

One day something *did* happen while McCarthy was serving what he viewed as his purgatory in the tow squad.

There was an incident at the exit gate of the impound lot near the Lincoln Tunnel. The people whose cars had been towed could show up at the impound lot, pay their fine and reclaim their autos. Provided, of course, there was anything left of their cars.

The night McCarthy made his bones in the tow squad, one of those unhappy, irate customers had attempted to run the barricade at the gate without paying. In the process he ran down a cop and nearly killed him.

"This is a hit-and-run, right in front of me. I take off. In pursuit. This is at Fifty-sixth Street and Twelfth Avenue. The guy goes across Fifty-sixth Street, down to Ninth Avenue, makes a right turn on Ninth, starts traveling south, and I start chasing him in the tow truck. I was going about sixty miles an hour in this old piece-of-shit tow truck. I was winding out the gears—it's not exactly an emergency vehicle.

"He turns down Forty-first Street, and I thought he was going through the Lincoln Tunnel. I go around the corner and start racing, but suddenly, I don't see the car anymore. And I stop.

"Behind me there's three parked cars; I back up and he's the third car. The guy had turned the corner and pulled over on me. So I jump out of the car, I get my gun out, and I go up to the car and the guy had the window open, and the next thing I know, I'm dragging him out of the car through the window. He's resisting all the way.

"There was a sanitation man who was sweeping the street there in front of this real skel bar; nobody in there except vagrants and lowlifes. He has one of those little carts with the garbage pail in it.

"Now, I get this guy out of the window and I'm trying to handcuff him on top of the hood of the car, and he's resisting.

The gun is no good to me. I can't use it and I'm afraid he'll get it off me and use it on me.

"But, I know this sanitation man is there. I say, 'Here, take this.' And hand him my gun.

"This is a cop-hater's bar. You go down the stairs. It's like in the cellar of this building. We'd had all sorts of problems there before.

"All these people start filing out of the bar—they're winos, street people, buzzards, lowlifes. They really are skeletons. Scumbags, street urchins; they're white, black; their teeth are rotted. And they're watching the fight and they're rooting for the other guy. Meanwhile, I think this whole thing is a setup because when I pulled this guy out the window, he's a black guy and I swear to God he looked like Sammy Davis, Jr. Just like him. And I start to look around for a camera.

"But I'm wrestling around. I glimpse out of the side of my eye that this sanitation man wants to drop dead. He wants to get out of there. The crowd is screaming at him; he's staring at the gun. The gun is pointed at me. They want him to shoot me. And I know I have made a terrible error.

"Finally, I get the guy handcuffed and I get the gun back, and the crowd is still screaming and yelling, and I get out of there as fast as I can. I throw the Sammy Davis, Jr. guy into the truck, take him into the station house and the cop who got run down isn't hurt too badly, so I let him take the collar.

"I stayed in tow service till I made sergeant. I was there for over three years. I started sergeants school the first week of January 1972, right after the Knapp Commission hearings on channel thirteen; Serpico, that whole thing.

"We were the first group from the academy to be selected under the Knapp guidelines. We were what they wanted the police to become."

SIX

Loyalty in the police department means you're willing to lie for someone else. Loyalty to me meant that I would always be the way I promised to be for another person. I would never be an ambush. Any person I worked with, I had to tell them right away that I wasn't on any pad. They had to know from me that if I caught them stealing, *I* would be the one to lock up their ass.

MOTHER'S MAXIM

███

THE KNAPP COMMISSION, 1970

An honest cop, a short, swarthy, intense detective named Frank Serpico—whom Bill McCarthy knew of from the old 7th Division, plainclothes, in the Bronx, but never a cop he worked beside—caused the formation of the Knapp Commission in late 1970.

By then, McCarthy was beginning his fifth year as a policeman; to the old-timers, to cops with twenty-five or thirty years, that meant he was still a rookie.

Serpico's disclosures about corruption ended his own police career prematurely and nearly cost him his life. As a graphic, eye-opening instructional tool for America, however, the value of the moody detective's shocking testimony could hardly be overestimated.

Serpico compelled people to accept the existence of systematic corruption in precisely the same way that Joe Valachi had convinced skeptics, a generation earlier, that the Mafia was an embedded fact of life in the United States.

The pervasiveness of rotten police apples inside the NYPD had never seriously been doubted. Before Knapp, there were the Kefauver Committee hearings in 1951, the Seabury investigations thirty years before that, and the original inquest into NYPD wrongdoing, the Lexow Committee, which began investigating in 1894. As a direct fallout of Knapp, there were follow-up probes in New York and in every other big city in America in the ensuing years.

However, police apologists, clinging to the moldy mythology of cops and cop-groupies, insisted that the thieves were individual perpetrators and that corruption was not system-wide. Insiders knew that such a benign scenario had never been the case. Cops were either "grass eaters" who passively accepted whatever cash fell their way, or "meat eaters" who actively put the bite on any hand they saw. Either way, a slack system tolerated them.

"Back when I broke in in Harlem and Brooklyn, during the riots, one of my first partners was picking up money, with me in the car, and I never even knew it. Had no idea. He was as corrupt a cop as I ever met. He was taking bookmakers' money, gamblers' money, pimps' money, right in front of me. And I just thought he had good community relations with the black people. I was that naive. That's when I first saw how the pad worked.

"Everyone would shake his hand and lean in the car and talk to him. Of course, they were giving him money and I never knew it. I thought they just wanted to see him, they'd come over to the car to say hello. I thought that was wonderful. And he loved to have me in his car because he didn't have to split it. It was a great deal for him.

"This guy had been on the job twenty-odd years. That's what I couldn't understand. I used to say, 'With all the seniority you've got, you can go anywhere. Why don't you ask for Queens or someplace?' And he'd say, 'Oh, no. You'll love it here. You'll see.'

"There wasn't even a decent place to eat in that precinct, but these cops refused to transfer. They were pulling down too much on the pad. To them, it was beautiful.

"I used to pay six dollars for a hamburger—22 West 135th Street. It was the Black Muslim restaurant. They hated me, but I said, 'I got money, I'll pay.' I used to go and sit in their restaurant and I was the only cop eating decent food. Everybody else was eating fried pork and chits. And it only cost a quarter. A lousy quarter. But that wasn't what they charged a cop.

"When I had two years on the job I went up against a plain-clothes cop who had sixteen. Very cool, streetwise, always wore suits. He was another crook. He was making money. We were in a regular patrol car over on the East Side. He was driving and I was the recorder, as they say.

"He said to me, 'Hey, kid, go get me a sandwich.'

"Now, what he was saying was, go into that store over there and get me a sandwich—for free. But I wouldn't do it.

"I got out of the car on Lexington Avenue, at about Sixty-Fourth Street, walked around to the driver's side, opened the door and yelled at him to get out of the car.

"He started to give me a hard time and I dropped my gun belt right in the middle of the street. I said, 'Now if you want to get back in this car, you have to get past me to do it.'

"He couldn't railroad me because he knew that I would tell what he wanted me to do. I would have gone on the six o'clock news with it.

"The outcome of that incident was: one, that I drove that car back to the station house *alone*. I left him standing there, on Lexington Avenue. And two: I got the point across that I had no time for peer pressure and all that police-code-of-silence bull. As far as I was concerned, a crook was a crook. I'd lock up a cop just as soon as the next guy."

* * *

[44]

Frank Serpico and others, like Sergeant David Durk, his confidant and contact with the world above ground during his long undercover entombment, effectively killed the myth of the honest police aristocracies. Any cop, of any rank, was open to a payoff, under any circumstances. That was the shameful reality of police life as the Serpicos, the David Durks, and later, the Bill McCarthys, discovered it.

Many small bands of bright, capable cops—frequently the best cops—had, in effect, become the most feared and efficient shakedown crews in a city already conspicuous for graft.

The cops raised the protocol of extortion from art to science. "Pads," or bribe schemes, existed everywhere, on every level, in every borough. Almost any cop in any part of New York could collect an extra thousand dollars a month or more, simply by looking the other way.

Building contractors who were used to paying off Mafia soldiers and associates to ensure labor peace claimed that payoffs to the police amounted to another mob tax on top of their standing illicit obligations, and told the Knapp Commission that bribes to the NYPD increased the cost of the average construction project in New York by as much as 5 percent. The Mafia itself could not pretend to be doing much better than that.

That two-year investigation, pushed rapidly by the reform mayor, John Lindsay, changed the New York City Police Department forever. Its methodical, precinct-by-precinct exposure of massive, structural corruption demonstrated the alarming vulnerability of a police force that had become impervious to outside inquiry and as clannish and hierarchical as the Ottoman Empire. Before Knapp, cops took other cops seriously. Period. Civilians didn't count. There was no unbolting of the heavy doors masking that closed blue society of incomparably dangerous, devious men, gifted men capable of breathtaking artifice.

When political expediency forced the Knapp Commission's final report to be made public in 1972—probably well before the commission's true work had been finished—there was evidence to suggest that half a million dollars a year were being pocketed by rogue cops. Nearly all of that money originated with the five traditional organized crime families of New York and eventually worked its way down to the cop on the street, through successive layers of hangers-on, go-betweens, and bagmen.

Usually, the money went to protect highly profitable prostitution or narcotics operations. Sometimes, the cops acted as mercenaries for the vice lords who were paying them. When they assumed these roles, the cops would be called on to arrest rival racketeers or merely serve as muscle whenever and wherever they might be needed.

"You didn't have to do anything overtly illegal to get put on a pad. All you had to do was go out and bang the balls off of whomever the hierarchy identified. Go knock over Harry's gambling operation. You were just doing your job, as far as you cared. That didn't mean that Harry's joint wasn't worthy of being knocked over, either. Because all the gamblers were bad, all the bars ran whores and drugs.

"The only line that most cops would have drawn was between the honest guys who just made their observations of illegal activity and took it from there—and you could *always* find something illegal—or the dishonest cops who flaked people, who planted phony evidence like dope or numbers slips. You could come up with all the evidence you needed—legitimately—even though the investigation itself might be part of some larger shakedown scheme that a captain or lieutenant had ordered.

"Now, why did the higher-ups identify that particular place—Harry's joint, for example—for you to go out and knock over in the first place? Why—because they were being bribed to do it. By *whom* was always the big question. More than likely, it would be some organized crime guy who wanted to hurt his competition. But the competition was breaking the law anyway, so even though it might have been selective enforcement, even good cops didn't have a big problem with it.

"A shakedown was known as making a guy good. If you made

him good, you made him pay you off, either to stay in business or for services rendered."

The extent of the institutional corruption was so vast and so unsettling, even to reformers like Patrick V. Murphy, the enlightened New York City police commissioner, that the attitude of most cops was to turn sullenly inward, in a state of genuine shock, and brand the investigation a witch-hunt that violated even the most basic civil rights of the targeted cops. And, a strong case could be made that the snowballing investigation did, in fact, degenerate into exactly that. Regardless of the way in which a suddenly vengeful criminal justice system decided to retaliate against allegedly crooked cops, however, the existence of the corruption itself could not be debated. Certainly not by people like Bill McCarthy.

Though painfully embarrassed, Murphy's office cooperated, and even launched an aggressive purge of its own, as did a succession of different district attorney's offices.

However, even the lowest-level players on the street could have saved the prosecutors' time and energy.

They knew the cops; they knew the rules. Any arrest, no matter how bad, could be squared for the right price. Manhattan dope dealers had long favored a two-thirds/one-third arrangement. If caught and busted, two thirds went to the cops on the take and one third was retained for sale. Any out-of-pocket loss would merely be passed on to the eager junkies in the jacked-up price of the dope. That was capitalism. Everybody stayed happy—including the cops.

Both the public and the press were unprepared for the Knapp findings. The degree of organization that fueled the bribe-taking was stunning. Even hardened prosecutors were amazed by the casualness with which cops, routinely, picked up payoffs *every* time they went out on patrol. In fact, it became apparent that many cops went out on patrol for the express purpose of collecting payoffs and for no other reason. McCarthy had witnessed all that as early as his rookie summer in Harlem.

McCarthy would eventually work with David Durk in the Organized Crime Control Bureau. There, they attempted to shanghai the best detectives from each other; men they could trust. Their job, in part, was to do battle with the corrupt, old-boy NYPD system.

Another central figure in the Serpico saga was a sympathetic inspector, Paul Delise, known as Saint Paul because he was a straight cop who would have nothing to do with the pads.

Saint Paul became the first superior officer to publicly back Serpico's resolute efforts to expose the pad system in Manhattan as he had done in the Bronx. In fact, when Delise realized that no other cops would serve as Serpico's partner, preferring to freeze him out, Delise told him not to worry; they would jump all the rules, all the traditions, all the department protocol against an officer of inspector rank (a full two steps above a captain) serving with a mere plainclothesman—and Delise became his partner.

Already fifty, long out of foot-pursuit shape and a desk-bound administrator for many years, Delise still hit the street with Serpico, chasing the bad guys, taking down the felony arrests and, in the process, so risking his own life as a matter of principle and professional pride that Serpico would later confide that he was sometimes more worried about Saint Paul than about the investigations.

McCarthy already knew how infected and influenced the police department could be by graft, but as part of that untouchable Saint Paul crowd, he also witnessed the metamorphosis that principled cops could bring about.

As long as a kid like McCarthy could avoid being blinded by the light, by all the glamor, by all those blinking, constantly running marquees that he saw whenever he closed his eyes, he might have a chance to make it.

That was a wide-open, never-to-be-duplicated era of giants in the NYPD, controversial supercops like Serpico, like Eddie Egan, who would be immortalized as Popeye Doyle in *The French Connection.*

Some of those people would end up working with McCarthy

or for him; gung-ho, nitty-gritty, investigative types. Detectives who went out and made their cases—classic lone wolves.

In reality, however, a detective needs constant direction. He's told what to do, when to do it, and how; he may, in certain cases, be very tenacious and stay on a case longer than most people would give him credit for. He might even be lucky enough to break the case, but without exception, he has to have a lot of organization behind him. That was where they intended the Bill McCarthys to come in.

The detectives could start the balls rolling, but they could only roll so far. The organization refused to allow its prima donnas just to run off in all kinds of directions. It had been burned too many times before.

The tough street guys were essentially lower-level investigators and somebody had to control them in every unit, set the tone. That was what had been lacking, those honest, enlightened field commanders who could actually *lead* their best investigators and establish an intensity level of both integrity and performance.

With McCarthy, you were never at a loss for direction. He would become the most recognizable prototype of the post-Knapp cop in the NYPD, swept along by the momentum of the reform, responsible for the probity of his team and, eventually, in command of the most sensitive beat in New York—Vice.

"There were so many innocent things that were all part of the corruption syndrome—like food that you could eat for free, coffee and buns and the newspapers. All the drivers on the newspaper trucks had sample copies that they carried around to give out to the police. They were marked "bad" because they had a little red dye on them. The *News, The Mirror, The Post,* they all delivered papers to the police. The milkman delivered milk to the police. The bread man delivered bread to the police. And there was nothing hidden about it. It was acceptable. It was not corruption.

"But, in addition to that, the cops were all down with the

gamblers. All the corruption was systemized and the only thing that I was ever told by my uncle—who was a cop—was that 'you're not gonna be a detective; you're not gonna go into plainclothes; you're not gonna be a boss. Study. You're not gonna be no detective, because being a detective is how you learn to steal as a cop.'

"It's a boss's job. That's what my uncle was trying to tell me. Why? Because you could tell other cops what to do and get paid for it. That's heaven for a cop. And even if you are corrupt, you get a bigger cut as a boss. That is a sacred tradition in the NYPD.

"In those days whatever a cop's quota was, his pad, his dirty money—a cop's share was a thousand dollars and a sergeant's share was a share and a half, fifteen hundred; a lieutenant got two shares, that's two thousand, a captain got three shares, three thousand, and so on all the way up. That's how it was. It was a boss's job. You made more money and had less risk.

"Naturally, as soon as I made sergeant, in March 1972, and much to my uncle's regret, they promoted me to plainclothes. There was no hotter spot in the entire NYPD.

"After Knapp, they wanted brand-new, clean, sanitized, threatened sergeants on probation. They took thirty-five of us out of a class of one hundred. We were supposed to be the cream of the crop because we were the youngest cops in the history of the department to pass the test for sergeant. We were told that we had the highest IQs; we were the best-educated group ever and, presumably, we hadn't been around long enough to have become *too* corrupted. That was our major attraction.

"Seniority was normally forty percent of what it took to get promoted to sergeant. Twelve years to make sergeant was average. I did it in five. I can thank the Knapp Commission for that. Now, with all the outside politics involved in the police department, they make sergeants in about twelve minutes— and they're all kids. Back then, though, it was a much bigger deal than it is today.

"As part of the indoctrination they threatened the shit out

of you: You're going to jail if you take a dime. That was the message. They were trying to make an individual commander's ass pucker with a concept called accountability. They created internal checks to test people. These were all recommendations of the Knapp Commission to prevent corruption in the future.

"They were imposing additional responsibility on new sergeants like myself so that if anybody on our teams did anything wrong, we were going to go to jail with them.

"They were going to try to impose all these controls and make a sergeant the man in charge. From that point on, a cop couldn't make a collar without a sergeant being present and being responsible. That meant making sure that no money changed hands. Before that, they just had to make the quota any way they could: five misdemeanors and two felonies a month.

"I arrived in the most provocative, interesting place in the whole world. At precisely the right time. In Vice."

SEVEN

The *Sergeant* had all the real power on the street.

MOTHER'S MAXIM

■

PUBLIC MORALS, VICE, 1972

One day in late March 1972, just before graduation, as McCarthy was leaving the academy to head downtown, he found Captain Kenneth Gussman waiting outside the classroom for him—the very same officer whom he had once accused of being corrupt.

The visit was unofficial, Gussman assured him, but important. McCarthy had no idea what was coming.

In sergeants school he had earned high enough marks in the leadership area to make several commanders around the city aware of him, and his hard-nosed proclivities. McCarthy just assumed that Gussman was among them. They didn't have any particularly close relationship, just a mutual respect.

Many other sets of interested fingerprints had also been left on McCarthy's file. He had recently earned his bachelor's degree from John Jay College, at night. It was a culmination of the degree work that he had interrupted to marry Millie and join the police department several years before. Not only that, but McCarthy had also launched his pursuit of a master's degree. Not many other people in the entire police department could make the same claim. Gussman was aware of all this because he had been doing his homework.

He knew, for example, that McCarthy's preference then was Narcotics, where plenty of smart cops were looking to get their career tickets punched. But Gussman also realized that McCarthy would have little say in the matter of his next job. Still, Gussman decided to meet McCarthy that day more as a recruiter than as a superior officer.

As the two cops walked outside together, the captain bought McCarthy a hot dog and soda for lunch—no cigarettes, this time. Then, as they strolled under a pleasant ocher sky, Gussman steered them away from the academy grounds on the East Side at Twentieth Street. As they walked, Gussman explained that what he had to tell McCarthy was best said out in the open, away from both listening devices and eavesdroppers.

Gussman then laid out his problem: While McCarthy had been working his way up and out of Traffic, and into sergeants school, Gussman had been attempting to do the same thing for himself. And he had succeeded. His new assignment was as the commanding officer of the new Public Morals Division, Vice, in the recently christened Organized Crime Control Bureau. This newest wing of the enormous NYPD infrastructure was the bureaucratic response to the anticorruption recommendations of the just-completed Knapp Commission.

No one could claim to truly understand the rune stones of the New York Police Department. You could spend a lifetime trying to interpret them and still miss a central passage. Duplicity was a commonplace.

The OCCB was a controlled experiment in widespread reform. Both McCarthy and Gussman, based on their own experiences, had reservations about how realistic or practical this new approach could be, but it did present a rare opportunity for police work without interference. McCarthy was intrigued.

"This was an institutional reaction against the time when the plainclothes cops, the detectives, had been renegades. They were running around doing whatever they wanted. All anybody had cared about prior to Knapp was making things good for the pad, taking in enough bribe money to go around.

"Right after the Knapp Commission when you had to be

[53]

honest, when they demanded that cops be scrupulous, that was like the promised land for me, with my altar-boy religiosity. I could hear my mother whispering in my ear again."

Even though the OCCB had been set up for the express purpose of hothouse-nurturing the new, supposedly corruption-free sergeants as role models for their men, the traditional NYPD hierarchy was imposed on top of that. And that's what had Kenneth Gussman worried enough to seek out Bill McCarthy. But, from the outset, the chain of command and the mechanism for ensuring ethical behavior among the cops seemed murky.

There was, for example, a lieutenant over every sergeant, and captains or inspectors over those lieutenants. An almost uncountable number of those senior officers still belonged to the bad old world of pads and payoffs. They regarded the Knapp Commission and its new disciples as mere obstacles, as the enemy. They had every intention to keep on doing all the illegal graft-taking that they had been doing.

Within the new Organized Crime Control Bureau there were to be almost autonomous, competitive subdivisions—Narcotics; Public Morals, where Gussman had been sent; Field Control (which was really Internal Affairs, cops who spied on other cops); and the Administrative Division, meaning intelligence and wiretaps.

This made little sense from a management point of view (forget the potential for civil rights violations; the cops were still reeling from Supreme Court decisions like the rulings about issuing *Miranda* warnings at the time of an arrest), but managers weren't running the show; cops were running it and they happened to be panicked, frightened cops at that.

Within this maze of bureaus and divisions, the most volatile area was the Pimp Squad, one of the traditional mother lodes of police payoffs and shakedowns. It had always been the ideal place for even sharp cops to get jammed up.

Captain Gussman needed someone running the Pimp Squad

whom he could trust—really trust. He needed a hardhead like Bill McCarthy, a man who was simply too proud, too stubborn, too sanctimoniously bent on doing the right thing even to consider taking a note. And that's exactly what he told the new sergeant.

Gussman believed in him, in his honesty. That long, argumentative night they had spent together years before—arguing over corruption and a damn pack of cigarettes—had convinced him. McCarthy was the only guy the captain wanted.

After he had offered the job to McCarthy, Gussman fell silent. Their walk had taken them all the way to midtown, a distance of several miles. While McCarthy thought it over, Gussman sat on a park bench and lit up a cigarette. The moment he caught McCarthy looking at him disapprovingly as he puffed away, the captain immediately tossed the burning stub into the bushes.

McCarthy smiled in approval. Then he thought some more about what Gussman was offering him: the chance to run a clean squad.

There would be unprecedented risks in this arrangement. For one thing, Gussman was a Jew and the NYPD was one of the most thoroughly anti-Semitic organizations on earth. As soon as the other cops in Public Morals realized why Gussman had selected him to run the Pimp Squad, there would be suspicion, jealousy, even accusations that McCarthy was no better than another Serpico.

But then he remembered something that Millie had once confided to him. When she was a little girl, and years later, as a grown woman partying in Spanish Harlem's notorious after-hours clubs, she had witnessed too many police payoffs. It always went the same way: The cops would walk in, slap a few people around, maybe grab a bar-girl's ass and expect to be taken care of. Being taken care of could mean anything from a blow-job in the back room to free drinks, and invariably, money would change hands. Then they would walk out, to utter silence. And the more recklessly they abused their power, the more deeply her people hated them.

Even before they were married, Millie had put it to Bill in

the one way that she knew he would understand.

"I could never sleep with a man," she had told him, "who is spoken about the way the cops are spoken about after they leave from picking up their payoff money." And then she had fixed him with those same flashing dark eyes that he had first fallen in love with back at the bank.

McCarthy never forgot her warning. It was the one and only discussion that he and Millie ever had about cops taking bribes. But it was enough.

McCarthy glanced over at the bench and saw that Gussman was reaching for another smoke. The captain wanted an answer. He deserved one.

"How do I know that *I* can count on *you,* if I get in a jam?" McCarthy asked him.

Gussman struck his match. "I didn't send you out for cigarettes this time, did I?" Gussman answered.

McCarthy understood. Gussman was grinning at him.

"You just got your new Pimp Squad boss," McCarthy told him.

"I knew I had him all along."

Then, the two men shook hands on it.

McCarthy was first sent to the OCCB's Administrative Unit. That lasted a little less than two months. It was a desk assignment, learning how to read and write intelligence assessments, developing skill with wiretaps. Gussman decided that would be a good way to condition McCarthy for his new responsibilities.

The same day that he left that brief assignment to transfer into Vice, into the Pimp Squad, an older, embittered inspector, familiar with the lures and the prevailing climate of prosecuting cops, but totally unaware of the understanding that had been hammered out between Gussman and McCarthy, looked Sergeant McCarthy right in the eye and predicted warily, "Just wait, in three months you'll be back here—in handcuffs."

McCarthy walked out the door without saying good-bye.

EIGHT

Cops are recognizable. That's the essence of their profession. You can have no real home life as a cop. You can't even eat your lunch. Somebody in the restaurant is gonna say, "Look at the cop; he uses salt." And they all spend their day seeing if you pay for your food. Somebody's always gonna say, "Watch, the cop won't pay for his food." And even if you do pay for your food the person will say, "Yeah, but he didn't *have* to pay."

MOTHER'S MAXIM

◼

CENTRE STREET, PERMANENT CADRE

From March 1972 until December of 1976, McCarthy served in Public Morals as a sergeant.

He began in a cold, gray, government-issue office building at 137 Centre Street. When McCarthy worked days, he would have to go in and unlock the door, turn off an alarm connected to the central communication system and bring the place to life. Public Morals was on the third floor, Narcotics was up on the eighth—that's where McCarthy first met Bob Leuci, later to be afforded the Hollywood treatment as the *Prince of the City*. The Organized Crime Control Bureau, Administrative Division, was on the seventh. The School Patrol and assorted other city agencies like the License Bureau and Parking Violations were scattered throughout the rest of the place.

McCarthy's Pimp Squad was the only team in the city of New York that worked Vice from ten o'clock at night until six o'clock the next morning. That was the night life, the players' time—the most dangerous dark hours when corruption-prone cops had limitless opportunities to make money. The Pimp Squad had the run of the city—loose women, fast cash, and cocaine. He might as well have been the police commissioner.

The organizational chart called for one sergeant, like McCarthy, to tightly monitor a six-man team: one detective sergeant with six hand-picked helpers, some of whom were "white shield" plainsclothes investigators, and some of whom were full-fledged gold shield detectives.

McCarthy would have been known in the old days as a "five-borough man"; his jurisdiction included Manhattan, Queens, Brooklyn, Staten Island, and the Bronx. After Knapp, "five-borough man" was changed to "permanent cadre" in the headquarters division of a city-wide unit. But it still meant the same thing, and in the NYPD, it meant power under either designation.

Historically, as far as corruption was concerned, it also meant that McCarthy was in the best spot in the world to make the most money, dirty money, because he had the entire city to rob. He knew everything that was going on and his authority, even as a sergeant, superseded any local commander because he was Vice, permanent cadre.

"I'm told that in 1961, a sergeant where I worked—it wouldn't have been in the Organized Crime Control Bureau then, because that didn't exist yet; it would have been called the Police Commissioner's Confidential Investigating Unit or the Public Morals Administrative Division, but basically the same jurisdiction—would have gotten envelopes full of bribe money, money from the pad, shoved into his locker right through the vent. That's how wide-open it was. A sergeant could have expected about nine thousand dollars a month—a share and a half. A cop would have gotten six thousand; a lieutenant, twelve thousand—that's two shares. Most of the money would come from the gamblers."

During his first five years as a cop, McCarthy thought that any day he was going to quit. That had been the hidden agenda in virtually all of his career moves. As soon as he completed his college degree, he would be gone. But everything changed. Both his promotion to sergeant and his degree came more quickly than he ever thought they would. And then something else happened.

Millie got pregnant. She had told him while he was still on the sergeant's list. Suddenly, he needed money—real money. Not just for himself anymore; not just for the two of them. With the sergeant's raise he would be making more money than he could reasonably expect to make on the outside. From that moment on, the NYPD had him.

Once he settled into the strange routine of Vice, following the timely intervention by Gussman, McCarthy found himself getting *back* to the office to begin his paperwork at five o'clock in the morning. In the years to come, every aspect of his life would be literally turned inside out, even sleeping and eating.

McCarthy had never been a night person. Vice, however, gave him no choice in the matter. When most ordinary people were plowing into afternoon traffic, beginning the long commute home to the suburbs after a difficult day, McCarthy would become accustomed to just starting his shift as a creature of Manhattan's dark night. As a Vice cop. That underworld became his home and he learned to love it there—perhaps too much.

McCarthy, always a family man, lived in those distant suburbs too, with one wife, two beautiful kids, and a dopey dog. He didn't actually have a white picket fence, but he did have the mortgage that went with it.

Sometimes, McCarthy used to wish that he were going home with the commuters, going home to Millie and their children, to their good life in Sloatsburg. The two of them were still the kind of lovers who had to be touching each other before either one of them could fall asleep, her smooth thigh warm and soft against his.

Once, in the middle of Manhattan, at the corner of Thirty-third Street and Eighth Avenue, he stole up behind Millie and dropped to his knees, in uniform, and began kissing her, progressively working his way up her legs, feet to ankles to knees, as a gathering crowd watched and as Millie, mortified, tried to keep from slinking down a vent grating.

In another way, however, McCarthy sometimes felt as cut off from Millie, from Sloatsburg, as it was possible for a man to be. Vice had done that to him as it had to countless cops before him.

Putting it all in perspective like that made him realize that his house in Sloatsburg—and even Millie—was actually the part of him that was growing fainter by the hour; it was like some old wedding portrait that had been left in the sun too long, and he could see himself fading from the picture. That was scary. He hated to admit it, but there were times—the bad times, mostly—when there was just too much competition from his other Life: the street Life, the whores and the pimps and all the bubbling, percolating plots in the Life.

The pace wasn't exactly killing him, but it was changing him. Before very long, he was eating little and sleeping less; no more than three hours at a time. Exhausted or not, some internal body mechanism snapped him awake by one o'clock every day—then he would run to burn away the tiredness, to kill the lonely afternoons. Ten miles every day. Weights for half an hour in the gym; three hundred turns on the incline board; five hundred hand pushups; then the parallel bars. Boxing next. Punch the heavy bag for half an hour and then more running on an outside track—two and a half miles from his house to the track, five miles around, back home again, all in under two and one half hours.

After spending all night making collars, taking in prisoners for booking, maybe breaking into a house or night-spot to execute a search warrant, then writing up the incidents, he would then have to quickly shut himself down and prepare for the inevitable crash, for the long drive home.

If they told him to stay until six, to brief the day team that was just coming on, they really meant that he should hang around until seven or eight.

This continual yo-yoing of bodies and schedules and emotions and marriages exacted the sort of toll that often resulted in divorce, burnout, even suicide and drug addiction. McCarthy saw what it could do to the men he worked with. He tried not to face what it could be doing to him.

Once he finally did arrive home, after working all night, it might be nine-thirty or ten o'clock before he was ready to settle in. The house would be empty, Millie would be off somewhere, working, leading the normal life dictated by the natural progression of light and dark, of mothering and child-rearing.

Inevitably, McCarthy found himself withdrawing further from that natural order of things. Vice had its own rules, its own dislocated sense of time and place, of values and motives, even of day and night.

Working in the Life came to demand his full attention. In practically all ways, McCarthy's family was the loser. Although they understood what was happening to him, even though they could see the pressure that he was under, appreciate the danger, they sometimes found it hard to bring themselves to forgive him.

M I L L I E :
"In Sloatsburg we lived in a yellow house on Sheridan Avenue. I loved that house. I started my family there, brought my babies home to that house.

"It only cost thirty thousand dollars, but that was the limit of what we could afford. We would spend the next sixteen years there, make it through some good times and bad.

"Bill missed out on a lot of things and it just used to hurt me so to see it happening. Like things with the kids. Meetings, obligations, social functions with the neighbors and stuff like that. All the little problems the kids had getting along. He didn't have time for any of those. They weren't important. Only his cases seemed important. We felt shut out of his life at times.

"If something came up, I had to stop him dead in his tracks. I couldn't just let it go, and let it go. I would say, 'We have to talk. Just sit down and we'll talk or you're not getting out of this house.' I had to stop him or he would just go to the job and let it go.

"Then, when he would come home and play daddy to Christine, our daughter, or to Billy, our son, I would be resentful because I had been doing so much on my own. Usually by the time I felt that way, it had built up and up and I couldn't take any more. Then he would stop. But I always had to make him aware of it. He couldn't see that for himself. He would have to see my anger. I would have to do something to get his attention. But always, instead of acting out my resentment, I've told Bill about it. We've been able to talk. Most cops and their wives never talk.

"When I would grab him and say, 'Try to be home a little more,' it was basically for himself, as well as the children. I knew there were things he was missing out on that he wanted to be there for, but he would lose all track of the time.

"And the children. There were times, especially as they got older, when they seemed to have conflicting feelings about their father. They wouldn't pay that much attention to whether he was around or not. And I couldn't stand to see that because it hurt Bill so much. And that hurt me.

"So, it reached the point where we had a big fight one day. The kids, my daughter especially, still bring this up every once in a while. We don't have fights like that often and this one was a biggie. A screaming and yelling fight and slamming doors. I finally went into the shower because I had to go out; he left the house too and he slammed the door so hard, the house shook.

"He got in the car and he told me he didn't know where he was going to go. But he got right back out and went into the basement while I was in the shower. Then I went down and we talked.

"I really wouldn't like my son to become a cop. No way. Because now the job is even more dangerous than it was. And if my daughter, Christine, said that she wanted to marry a cop, I would have to sit her down and make her *really* understand what I went through, what she would be giving up.

"I used to have this recurring nightmare—that I kept missing an airplane. We were all supposed to be going on a trip somewhere, in this fantasy. Every night I would dream that Bill and the kids would get on the airplane in time, but I always missed it. And as it was taking off down the runway, I was yelling at the people in the airport to stop the plane—*stop it!* But they never did and I'd never make it."

NINE

*A **Dangerous Man** is one you can't predict. A man with
a gun, that's not danger, that's everyday.*

MOTHER'S MAXIM

THE TEAM, THE PIMP SQUAD

One of the main jobs of the Pimp Squad in the early 1970s was
policing after-hours clubs and Times Square. That was how
McCarthy broke in. It was the beginning of the upward crawl
of commercial sex and pornography from its oozing underground black market to the economic big leagues when, eventually, even the hardest-core sexually explicit loop would
become readily available in your friendly neighborhood suburban video store.

The six-man Pimp Team that McCarthy took over had a hard
time accepting him at first. He was only twenty-seven when he
started, loud and opinionated, and they were mostly older and
wiser and even more cynical. The only thing they knew for
certain about McCarthy, at first, was that he used to drive a tow
truck. They were ready to gobble him up.

The two most experienced members of the team were John
Gorman, a quiet, thoughtful cop who read hardcover books
and who happened to have a brilliant career ahead of him in
the police department, and Tony Vitaliano. Although both were
barely into their thirties then, they were already highly regarded
in Vice.

Through transfers and manpower problems, the makeup of

the teams in Public Morals was constantly shifting. Half the time, the sergeants, who actually ran things, just kept swapping problem children back and forth.

Tony Vitaliano—Tony-the-V was the Pimp Team's best undercover man. He looked more like one of the bad guys than the bad guys did—silk suit, thin shoes, a tiny gold horn around his neck. And a gun.

Normally his voice rasped as though he'd just swallowed a whole mouthful of East River sediment—sand, gravel, and bald tires. The way Tony barked he could have been hiding polyps the size of walnuts in his voice box.

Tony Vitaliano understood the Life by instinct. He had been born to it—right parents, right neighborhood, right relatives back in Sicily. He was just a tough cop from the South Bronx—and all that you could ever hope for in an Italian gangster, East Harlem, through and through. McCarthy always told the back-ups who didn't know Tony how to recognize him: "The guy who looks the baddest, that's the cop." Tony couldn't drink worth a damn—two drinks and Tony was loaded, they'd have to carry him out—and that was a liability, an undercover who kept getting falling-down drunk, but in Tony's case, he was worth it.

After a job, he would come back to the roach-trap office at 137 Centre Street, just a short walk from the Tombs, and type a whole report without a mistake. Amazing. And he'd do it with a throbbing scotch headache.

JOHN GORMAN:
"McCarthy seemed to be personally offended by what he saw in Vice, in the Life. It gave him the extra impetus, and being a supervisor, he could then translate that down to the group of men who worked for him and they would, in turn, reflect his personality and his method of operation, and that's pretty standard in the police department. If you have someone who is apathetic and thinks things are okay as they are, you'll find

[65]

his men will reflect that attitude, too. Under McCarthy, our team went out and turned up excellent cases. We did a real hard charge on things that other people thought were less than important: like the abuse of child prostitutes in the Times Square area. *No one* was working that then, except McCarthy's guys. The rest of the police department was very cold about it, almost matter-of-fact. So the kids were being exploited, so what? A whores's a whore, regardless of the age. So where's the crime?

"Not McCarthy. *That* issue, commercial pedophilia, became his crusade, and, in turn, our crusade too.

"He was a damn good cop, a damn good man. He pushed it because of his own personal convictions, because it really outraged him, while a lot of other people would just sweep it under the rug and not want to see it. The feeling then was that it was just one of those so-called victimless crimes, but McCarthy raised the consciousness of the entire NYPD. And he received very little credit for it."

John Scarpa—Short, pudgy, not at all imposing; he couldn't do a sit-up. Seemed more like an insurance man than a cop. He already had the hollow look of burnout. But McCarthy had run into Scarpa a few times before, at the police academy, and he liked him. On the surface he might have appeared to be an underachiever, but McCarthy suspected that Scarpa could do anything he had to do. His strength was in his even, unflappable calm.

As soon as Scarpa realized how straight the new sergeant was he began to call McCarthy "Zondarel," which meant "saint" or "savior" in Scarpa's Italian dialect. The nickname began as a put-down; it didn't stay that way.

Harold Schiffer—Known universally as a "Jew who could fight." He was a competent, impatient investigator, one of the top 10 percent in Brooklyn South Public Morals. He was also an army veteran and a Zionist, practically a Judeo-phile. Schiffer was given to somber suits and trench coats; he exuded the brazen confidence of an old-time private eye. The minute Schiffer walked into a room he could transform it into a set for some *film noir*.

After the army, Schiffer had traveled to Israel where he volunteered for one of the forwardmost *kibbutzim* in Palestinian territory. His first week there, he later told people, he saw more action than during his entire U.S. Army tour.

Schiffer was from a neighborhood known as Pig's Town in Brooklyn; a hundred years before they used to slaughter pigs in his backyard. But nobody joked about it to his face.

He had been brought up in a very Orthodox home, with a grandmother who spoke only Yiddish and parents who were deaf. He went to school while he was in the police department and McCarthy used to help him with his homework.

Schiffer had never seen anyone as driven as McCarthy. He was always giving someone on the team what Schiffer liked to call his Sermon on the Mount. But that was just McCarthy's way, Mother's way. He was the best cop Schiffer had ever seen, the craziest cop in New York when it came to right and wrong.

At a black pimp bar on Second Avenue, the team once jumped a car that looked out of place; two white men, both known gamblers. The car was stolen and there were drugs inside.

While they were booking the prisoners one of the men from the car—a fresh hood with mob connections—happened to notice the name of the arresting officer, "Schiffer."

"What kind of name is Schiffer?" the gambler demanded. "You're a fucking Jew, aren't you? You're a Jew? I know why you're doing this. I probably stole your lunch money in the schoolyard. You mocky."

Schiffer, normally a pro, lost it that time. He blew up; the other cops had to drag him out of the station. He had taken his gun belt off and was ready to take the prisoner outside and fight him, one on one.

But no one was allowed to brutalize prisoners on McCarthy's team—whether they deserved it or not. It took some doing, but they finally calmed Harold down. But no one could ever forget the rage in his eyes.

About two months later, the gambler who had taunted Schiffer was shot to death, assassination-style, as he walked out of a restaurant called Separate Tables. The murder was never solved.

Schiffer, of course, had absolutely nothing to do with the hit, but the team always joked about it darkly; no one ever wanted to see Harold that mad again.

Mike Sullivan—Had a face and manner that made people think of Mugsy Maginnis from the old *Our Gang* comedies. A central casting New York detective. Small, ruddy-faced, hot-tempered and with a potbelly and bent nose that looked as though it had been broken at birth, Sullivan was known as *"Camarón"* in the Puerto Rican bars. That was the Hispanic slang for "shrimp"; all the Irish cops had soft pink skin that looked like a shrimp's.

Sullivan had been a high school math teacher before becoming a cop and that had made him immediately suspect in the anti-intellectual NYPD. But McCarthy liked him because Sullivan could take a punch. He turned out to be the back-down-from-nobody alley fighter that the team needed.

McCarthy had inherited both Schiffer and Sullivan from the Porno Team in Public Morals. That was a parallel unit within Vice that had a considerably higher profile within the department.

Schiffer had also come in under Captain Gussman, the man who had handpicked McCarthy for the Pimp job. Since both Gussman and Schiffer were smart, straight Jewish cops, and because the NYPD had traditionally been a virtual extension of the Archdiocese of New York, Schiffer had taken a bad rap, early on, from his Irish and Italian Catholic brother officers who frequently hated Jews as a reflexive carryover of their own upbringing. Schiffer was suspect as the captain's mole, or "field associate"—the term for departmental spies right after Knapp.

Following a run-in with his supervisor on Mulberry Street,

[68]

in Little Italy, after a botched mob surveillance, Schiffer had been forthwith exiled to McCarthy's Pimp Squad with this admonition from his previous commander: "The Jew bastard captain tried to put a fucking Jew on my team—now he's your problem, McCarthy."

Tough Mike Sullivan had been the victim of a similar clash with a boss. Sullivan had refused to back down. That was it for him. Both turned out to be two of the best detectives McCarthy could have asked for.

"When I walked into the Squad, the lieutenant there was a drunk. He used to drink with another guy on my team, Billy Webster. They'd pay for the booze on Webster's expense account—three hundred dollars a month as the chief intelligence gatherer for the team, which was a fortune in those days—and they always went to the same joint on Forty-seventh Street. It was all a scam. The only intelligence they gathered was from each other.

"Webster was a pretty bad guy from the Middle-West; I guess now you'd call him a white supremacist. He wore cowboy boots, carried a gun that looked like a cannon, and had dedicated himself to saving the NYPD from the Jews.

"Those two hooked up with another cop who had come on about the same time I did—and he was just as bad. Everything was a conspiracy with him. He imagined that somebody was always trying to stop him from doing the big case or preventing him from making the big arrest. The other two idiots convinced him that it had to be the Jews. So they automatically hated Schiffer and Gussman and they hated me more because I was in on it with the Jews. And, believe it or not, these weren't bad cops. They were very capable. But from day one, they did not want me there.

"Cops love to intimidate each other and these guys were prime examples of that. But it never worked with me.

"I had five fights with other cops and three were with bosses. Every one of them was a coward, a bully who was getting by because no one ever tested him. They got by on rank.

"There was one cop who used to cock his gun and chase a Jewish rookie I worked with around the locker room, for no other reason than the fact that he happened to be a Jew. That made me sick, it made me angry.

"I told this asshole to stop doing that and leave the Jewish kid alone. But he kept on doing it. So I grabbed his hand with the cocked gun, and I stuck the barrel in my mouth and I said, 'I'm gonna get you locked up for murder, you asshole.' That was such a shock that he backed down right away.

"I could see that my new assignment in Vice meant working with that kind of cop again. I had to take a stand right from the beginning.

"After my first month, Webster's expense account went from three-sixty down to forty-eight dollars. So he begins bad-mouthing me. I was no good; I would never work out; I was too educated; I didn't know how to talk to people, street people; I was a Jew-lover like Gussman. And they threatened to keep all the informants away from me.

"But that didn't scare me because I knew they were liars and drunks on top of that. And I knew their confidential informants were all a smoke screen for the boozing."

One night when he was in the Centre Street office by himself, shortly after McCarthy had started with the Pimp Team, one of those informants called in.

Immediately, he realized that he would have to win her confidence and put her at ease—all on the telephone, stranger to stranger.

She said she was a prostitute and so was her sister. He must have kept the line open for two hours, squeezing out every droplet of intelligence that he could gather, cajoling them, sweet-talking them, getting the message across that he wasn't a cop on the dark side.

What McCarthy didn't realize at the time was that Chief Paul Delise, Saint Paul, Frank Serpico's old comrade, had *also* been secretly listening in—trying to see what the new sergeant was made of. It was just one among the many games that were being played after Knapp.

As soon as McCarthy ended his conversation with the whore and finally started to put the phone down, another voice mysteriously came on the line—Delise's voice—and he said to McCarthy, "Sergeant, I want to speak to you after you have finished."

Delise had locked himself in the Public Morals office, in a room that they all thought was empty, and had remained in there from six o'clock in the evening until McCarthy had showed up at eight-thirty. He had been sitting in there in the dark, waiting for the Pimp Squad to come in, then he would begin eavesdropping, monitoring their phone calls searching for one honest cop.

Later, Delise, who was a very powerful presence at that juncture, said that he had been really impressed with the way McCarthy had handled the informant.

Then, like a spook, Delise simply left, disappeared into the night. No further explanations, no hint of his real purpose for being there.

For two weeks after that, everywhere McCarthy went he was convinced that Saint Paul was still following him.

TEN

The only way to survive in the police department is to
be anonymous, because if they can point you out for
some reason, then they can attack you. Cops operate
out of fear and jeopardy. In the police department,
Power is based on rank, not intelligence.

MOTHER'S MAXIM

Two weeks into the Pimp Squad, the lieutenant who hated him
encountered McCarthy on a Friday night and told him to go
out with John Scarpa and "have a quiet night." He was the
untested sergeant and Scarpa was another cop the lieutenant
didn't like or consider a heavy hitter. Already, McCarthy was
being frozen out and he knew it.

"We were like the lowlifes of his team—McCarthy and Scarpa.
In police talk, 'Have a quiet night' means 'Don't do nothing.'
So, okay, I'm not gonna do anything. But now, they have
me mad.

"I knew that Vice had been after this one particular pedophile for something like a year. But they hadn't done anything with him. At the time, he was probably the biggest—
by that I mean the most active, the most visible—pedo in
New York. His street name was Peter Big and he *was* big,
huge, maybe six feet five and three hundred pounds. Thick

[72]

glasses. If you wanted to make a cartoon of the typical pedo, the dirty old slobbering monster, this was your boy. But Peter Big had managed to get his cases wired every time the police had even come close. He was a Manhattan millionaire and appeared to be a legitimate businessman who ran his family's import/export company.

"It was time for me to try to make my bones with these cops if I was ever going to be able to get them to work for me.

"I take Scarpa with me and we go over to the old French Hospital on Thirtieth Street, between Eighth and Ninth Avenues. Peter Big was in the building right next to it. Very sedate, with gray granite and dark awnings and a wrought-iron railing outside. The place was still pre-war Manhattan.

"We observe all these kids trafficking into this apartment house. I see which bell they're ringing—sixth floor. The apartment is in the name of a Chinese doctor, but it's really Peter Big's place. This Chinese quack is a Dr. Feelgood for the Upper East Side beautiful people. He was like their private narcotics connection. Pills and all sorts of other prescription drugs. This was just a sample of the intelligence they had on these people, but guess what? No arrests had been made.

"Whenever this Dr. Feelgood makes a house call, somebody usually sends a limo or a private jet to pick him up. Peter Big had managed to nose his way into this circle because quite a few of the notables in it had the same sexual preferences as Mr. Big. So he actually pimped for them, too.

"The way it worked was, if you wanted him to import some rare silk for you, antiques, something like that, he could handle it. But, if you wanted a matched set of ten-year-olds, boys, who could speak no English, that was possible too. Feelgood made the introductions and cleaned up the messes.

"For whatever reason, the feds had ignored his activities despite the fact that much of it was interstate and offshore and should have, therefore, fallen within their jurisdiction. But that was an old story with them. The word was that somebody as high up as Washington, D.C., was a link in Peter Big's daisy chain, but we never knew for sure. That could have been nothing more than loose cop talk, but somebody had certainly enabled this pedo to live a charmed life.

"Collectively, the cops in Vice had developed a personal grudge against this pervert. He embarrassed them and kept reminding them that, as cops, minus any real political juice, they could only enforce the law up to a point.

"That night, during our surveillance, six kids come out together and they get in a car. John Scarpa turns around and says to me, 'Mr. Big is open for business.'

"I waited for the car to turn around the corner, then I said to Scarpa, 'Let's jump the car.' He looks at me like I just said, 'Let's set ourselves on fire.'

"With these cops, in that squad, where no one was ever around to take charge, this was revolutionary. Scarpa really gets excited; he's ready to charge. All of a sudden, he's out with a sergeant who wants to act like a cop, too. I don't care who he is, a cop gets revved up by that.

"We hit the siren, put the light out on top and cut in front of the kids in the car on Eighth Avenue.

"I jumped out and started lining people up against the car. Scarpa thinks he's in heaven. This is the real thing; we're acting like real cops.

"The car turned out to be hot—thank God, because I had no reason whatsoever to pull it over—and we lock up the six kids. Ordinarily, that would have been the end of it.

"But we take them all to the station house and start to question them. All six admitted that Peter Big had done blow-jobs on them. The oldest kid was thirteen. They're all between nine and thirteen. Now, I have the witnesses and the crime. Peter Big is going down.

"We go right back to the French Hospital neighborhood, just in time to see another kid going in. He takes the elevator. Scarpa stays downstairs and covers the exits while I run up the stairs and I hit the sixth floor just as the kid's getting off the elevator.

"I hid in the stairwell and waited. As soon as Peter Big opened the door to let the kid in, I was right behind them.

"The apartment looked like an Oriental bordello. There were these soft red lights in lamps with gold fringe. Expensive antiques everywhere.

"Peter Big sort of cowered, then just sat down on a divan and glared at me. He had on a long dressing gown and silk pajamas. Big, fat, soft hands, like velvet. He had the softest hands I ever touched. He didn't protest, just sort of simmered. But the expression on his face said it all: Let's just get this out of the way so I can get back to business. He would come downtown with me, make his phone call and get the pinch blown out.

"There were two more kids in there, in his bedroom. One was half naked and the other one had part of his shirt off, like he was getting comfortable. Just little kids, but ghost-eyed little kids. They took it all in stride, too. Neither one even made eye contact with me. When I first went in, I actually think they figured I was there for some action too. Just another customer. That's how casual it all was.

"Peter Big had his satin pillows all fluffed up at the head of his bed, the spread was turned down; the night table had a single candle burning on it and there were these little porcelain jars, just exquisite, with creams and lubricants in them. The whole room smelled so sweet I almost vomited.

"I locked him up, took him downtown. Then, I got a search warrant and came back to the apartment. We looked around and came up with 295 pills and a gun. Now, it's turning out to be a nice pinch. The pills could tie in the doctor, too. That could lead us to the rest of the pedo ring.

"I had separated the six original kids and questioned them; each kid described the sexual act that had occurred individually with Big. I would be able to prove that each one had been sexually abused because I could describe with such specificness the sexual act: Peter Big blowing the kid, taking the semen, spitting it into the kid's belly button, then licking it around on his stomach to make it look like a glazed donut. That was his thing. Later, we found out that he would use a razor to carve the kids' thighs with X's and other marks. He was a sadist and

[75]

was actually much more dangerous than we thought. The gun, for example, came as a complete shock.

"Peter Big had been collared before and was very slick. He had never allowed one kid to witness him having sex with another kid; that way no corroborating witness could testify against him. Plus, he knew the cops would lay off.

"This time, however, I got him good.

"The next morning, I check in with the stolen car, nine sex collars, all corroborated, a gun, and 295 pills. And Peter Big was the guy they had been working on and allegedly couldn't get. I guessed going in that I had just absolutely ruined somebody's day.

"The lieutenant gets me aside and lays into me. He was so mad he couldn't even get his breath. All he kept yelling was, 'Do you realize what you've done? Do you know how this is going to look?'

"What I didn't find out until years later was just how badly I had humiliated him. There I was, supposed to be this young whippersnapper, supposedly the youngest sergeant in the police department at the time; I knew nothing about plainclothes, and I had already been tagged as some kind of Honest John freak, a Knapp Commission guy all the way, who didn't belong *anywhere* in New York, and especially not in Vice. Yet me and Scarpa—the two lowlifes—had taken out this guy and had shown up the hotshot detectives.

"From that night on, the other Vice cops thought I might be worth listening to."

But McCarthy soon realized that there were no final victories in Vice.

The night after he arrested Peter Big, he drove past the old French Hospital again. It was just past midnight. The pedophile had already been released on bail. McCarthy watched as Peter Big, who appeared to be just getting home for the night, came hurrying out of the building's underground garage. The pedo's zipper was open and his pants looked disheveled. McCarthy

[76]

knew instantly that he had been someplace else with some other kid.

In the police department of McCarthy's early days as a Pimp Squad sergeant, a boss was not supposed to get involved in the action. That was why his direct involvement in the Peter Big case proved to be so eye-opening. Making arrests meant going to court, and if he was in court, then he couldn't be back at Vice directing the team. And every single team was decidedly sergeant-driven.

If one of the team members made a good collar and then had to go to court, though, that still left five men plus the sergeant. Nothing made McCarthy rebel more than this fuzzy concept since it denied any boss a meaningful leadership role. But that was the antiquated system that had evolved. Few bosses questioned it because it allowed them to avoid most of the danger, much of the work, and it always provided a scapegoat— the detective—for collars that went bad. But McCarthy just couldn't accept it. Almost immediately, and certainly following the Peter Big case, he developed a reputation as a sergeant who *would* get involved, no matter what.

Peter Big did allow McCarthy to make his bones, not just with the cops, but with the people on the street, too. One of the first vice operators to really check him out was an old madam known as Miss Cindy. She had *heard* what this new cop was made of, but she still had to *see* for herself.

At that time, "Miss Cindy" was believed to be the proprietress of the largest whorehouse in New York. She was Italian and connected. All five mob Families had used her girls. She paid off no one, surviving instead solely on the considerable strength of the services her young ladies rendered. No one, including Sydney Biddle Barrows, the Mayflower Madam who would later set herself up as direct competition for Miss Cindy, had developed a more impressive clientele.

McCarthy was introduced to her on the corner of Sixth Avenue and Fifty-seventh Street in midtown; she was cautious and afraid of wiretaps. That first meeting with her had to be open-air.

McCarthy pulled up in an unmarked car, parked, but didn't get out.

The old woman, dressed like any one of a hundred other New York dowagers out for a late afternoon stroll, approached McCarthy cautiously. She stared at him, appraising him as though he were one of her new girls. As she leaned against the door of his car and started talking to him, he felt himself tighten uneasily. McCarthy had to listen hard, there was traffic and street noises and no possible way to record anything that she was telling him. But that wasn't really his intention today; today he was courting her, like a kid standing inspection by his first date's mother.

Neither was what the other expected. McCarthy was surprised by how elderly she appeared, how frail, how thoroughly used up. Whoremongering was a brutal business, he couldn't understand how an old girl like this could survive. But she had—which meant that he still had a lot to learn.

For her part, Miss Cindy was more than a little put off. She'd heard stories and, frankly, this young sergeant didn't look as intimidating as she thought he would. Or should.

"The key person in any of these vice operations was the manager or madam. They functioned as the foreman. If a girl could only do fifteen or twenty guys a day before she broke down completely, the madam would try to push her into doing twenty-five. It was just piecework to them. What's another five johns? Another five dicks?

"I wanted to get her working for me because I knew she had broken in half of the most expensive hookers in the city. At that point, Vice was involved with the murder case of one of the guys targeted by the Knapp Commission. I had been ordered to try and find one particular prostitute whom this guy had arrested ten years earlier and who might have valuable information.

"I went from one madam to another until I was finally referred to Miss Cindy."

Still evaluating McCarthy, Miss Cindy told him about a girl who worked for her. The girl had run into some bad trouble with a pimp, Karate Jim; he'd beaten her up, put her in the hospital, ruined her looks and her earning power.

At no point did the old lady show the slightest compassion for the injured hooker. This was a business disagreement and a valuable piece of her property had just been practically destroyed. One of her busiest whorehouses was known as the Factory. The name fit, too.

Now, what was the new kid from the Pimp Squad going to do about her suddenly damaged goods? Her hands on her hips, her face twisted into a rouged question mark, Miss Cindy waited for an answer.

McCarthy felt all of his instincts pulling him back to the elimination basketball games at the Maguires' schoolyard in Rockaway. Miss Cindy had winged a ball straight for *his* face, and now she was watching for him to flinch. Miss Cindy didn't give a damn about the law, about judges or the courts. All she was interested in was swift, certain street justice. Would McCarthy be man enough to handle that?

"I told her to tell the girl to get in touch with me as soon as she was able. I was going to lock up Karate Jim the minute I laid eyes on him.

"'No,' she says, 'he's bad.'

"I knew I had to send out a message right here.

"You tell him I want to meet him. He's supposed to be a karate expert. Well, so am I. And I want him. I want him bad.

"I actually happened to be taking karate lessons at that time. I knew I wasn't any good at it, but I could talk my way out of anything.

[79]

"Then, I jumped out of the car—she thought I was going after her—and I did a vicious side-kick right there on Fifty-seventh Street in the middle of traffic, really snapped out a kick.

"I said to her, 'You tell him that's what I'm gonna do to him.' I couldn't sense if she was impressed or not. But I wasn't about to vacillate; she had to know—and then had to spread the word—that I was prepared to carry through with exactly what I said I would do.

"Two hours later, I go down to a pimp bar where I think I might find this Karate Jim. And I have to admit, I'm a little shaky myself. I figured it would be a fight, but, win or lose, at least I could get it over with.

"I go into the place, it's already smoking. The word had gotten out that this crazy sergeant from the Pimp Squad was out to get Karate Jim—*this psycho is a trained killer,* that's what they were saying already.

"At least I had one question answered. I guess I did impress Miss Cindy.

"In the bar now they're coming up to me: 'I understand you're looking for Jim; he ain't here, we heard he left town; Jim don't want to die, man.' All this stuff.

"I figure I'm nuts not to roll with it. I say, 'Yeah, you tell Jim I'm gonna kick his pimp ass. No pimp is safe touching a woman in New York. That's my job. Every working girl out there is *mine* now. This is my turf now. Anybody beats on another whore, I beat on him. Jim *insulted* me.'

"I'm coming on with all this macho act. And believe me, it *was* an act. Nobody's even challenging me; why not?

"So what happens? The guy actually *does* leave town. I find that out the very next day. And remember, I have never so much as *seen* this Karate Jim.

"Then, a week later, the story gets even bigger. They got me having *killed* this Karate Jim; that's why he's not around any-more. I'm bad. And what had I actually done? I had jumped out on Fifty-seventh Street in front of some old madam and kicked at the air. That was it. But that was also enough.

"I learned a valuable lesson. You have to convince them that you are crazier than they are. That's how you get away with it. Then, you just wait for the results to come in.

"The Karate Jim thing took off. Even with the cops. They were no different from the people in the pimp bar. Somebody repeated a story and they believed it. Then the cops would pass it on with *their* embellishment.

"A little while after that I actually did have to go and serve a subpoena on this black guy who owned a karate studio. Obviously, he *was* the real thing.

"It's nighttime and I go in; the whole studio is just lit with candles. Creepy.

"I look around. Don't see anything, don't hear anything. Then, all of a sudden, they start to drop out of the ceiling on me. And these guys *were* karate experts. They jumped all around me in the candlelight. They all must have been perched up on the rafters like cats on shelves.

"They really came at me. All this kung fu stuff. I'm just swinging back, like in a barroom brawl. This is one of the worst fights I've ever seen and I'm in the middle of it.

"At my karate school, as an exercise, they used to turn out all the lights and beat you with a bamboo stick. That was a normal part of the training. But it was just in school.

"This was the first time I ever had to try it for real. So I just started kicking back and screaming out all the words I knew in Japanese from class. I had to make them think I knew a lot more about this than they did.

"And it worked. *Again.* Another bluff. They backed down and I finally got them under control. I even served the papers. If only they knew.

"I go back to the station and the story's like a miniseries by now: *Did you hear what McCarthy did this time? He took out a whole karate school.*

"After that, when I'd have trouble in a bar, and a guy would want to fight me, I'd get this crazy look on my face and start to scream and punch myself, I'd slam myself right in the head: YOU WANNA FIGHT ME? YOU WANT TO? COME ON, COME ON! LET'S GO!

"And he wouldn't want to fight anymore. That's theater. But I really did punch myself. 'I'm ready. I'm willing to go. No problem. I'm ready.' Then, I'd calm down and say, 'Hey, I feel like somebody just punched me.'

"I wanted to get to the point where I could just turn on the switch. And I worked at it. I'm a guy who *practiced* going nuts. I became deliberate as hell about it.

"In the meantime, I'm winning over Miss Cindy. I found out that she thought she was getting arrested. Now, you would have thought this old girl was somebody's grandmother. Her apartment was full of plants. She'd just walk around in there in these very expensive dressing gowns, watering her plants all day. But in the back of her head, she's worried about doing hard time. A woman in her seventies, at least.

"All the time I'm still trying to get her to put me in touch with the prostitute from ten years ago who figured in the murder investigation.

"The next time I see her, Miss Cindy is in a restaurant on Fourteenth Street, on the East Side, Irving Place. She's eating truffles. And hyperventilating. Something really had her agitated.

"Now she was a true organized crime madam, as opposed to a phony who only claimed to be protected by somebody high up. The wiseguys loved her stable. It seemed like nobody of any consequence could get laid in New York unless Miss Cindy had a piece of the action. That went right from the political big shots all the way down to a social club in Brooklyn.

"She was sharp, too. For a long, long time she had never even taken a collar.

"At that time there were only three Chinese cops in the police department. She knew them all by sight. Now, she also happened to have one of her houses that catered to Asian clients exclusively, mostly Chinese. Because she knew the three Asian cops they could never get near the place. So it was practically impossible to bust her for that house.

"She wanted another favor. She had a partner with whom she had had a falling out. The partner managed the Chinese house. But the partner was sloppy; she would allow Caucasians to come in when she was on the door. That was her beef. The partner wasn't careful enough. Sooner or later, she was afraid that the partner would allow a Caucasian cop to come in and that would be it.

"I was supposed to go in as a customer and arrest the partner for running a house of prostitution. Take her out of the picture. Sort of a preemptive strike. In return, I would get what I wanted from Miss Cindy. She never attempted to bribe me; it was strictly on the basis of exchanging information.

"I got that cleared with Vice, went in with a couple guys and made the pinch. It was quite a scene. All these Chinese guys were running around half-dressed, diving under beds, crying, and the girls were naked, pulling the covers up over themselves; everybody's yelling in Chinese. And over in the corner there's a television on; I think it was a kung fu movie.

"It didn't take long for Miss Cindy to deliver. She came up with the prostitute we wanted from ten years back and Homicide was able to question her about the murder of a plainclothes cop who had figured prominently in the investigations undertaken by the Knapp Commission. That hooker turned out to be one of our most reliable sources. You just can't have too many people from the Life who are willing to talk to you."

Miss Cindy became one of McCarthy's best introductions into the glamorous side of vice, the "high-priced spreads," as they called the expensive hookers. One of the most useful things that he picked up from her, and from her Chinese connections, was a sense of just how specialized the whorehouses could be. The variations—in terms of sexual services offered or the kinds of women employed or the ethnic groups and tastes that were catered to—led to just the sort of intelligence that he was hoping to find.

ELEVEN

The average *Prostitute*, if you were to strip her naked, is bruised, abused, her plumbing leaks, and her underwear is stained. It would be like screwing a jar of pus. And you shouldn't screw what you wouldn't kiss.

M O T H E R ' S   M A X I M

On a good night, the Pimp team would hit four or five pimp bars and "visit" three or four after-hours clubs.

Often, they doubled as warrant-servers for the Porno Squad, working the day shift, crashing peep shows, live sex emporiums, and adult bookstores. They would count on three collars at each spot—the two guys working the floor and the one guy "on the stick," at the door.

Following the pimps took McCarthy's men to the kinds of bars, the after-hours clubs, where you could still buy a drink past four in the morning. The clubs were open everywhere—midtown, Chinatown, Little Italy, wherever there was sex or gambling.

In appearance, they could be anything from plush to pedestrian, from dignified old supper rooms to degenerate dives. No one, including the Vice cops, could ever spot the after-hours clubs from the outside. The owners went out of their way to make sure that every building facade or location retained that run-down New York look. However, once you were inside, you usually had to go up in an elevator, or down into the basement or through a front operation into the back room. There was always some kind of improvised fortification, like a steel door, and frequently, a Pete-sent-me porthole.

One of McCarthy's search warrants was aimed at locating a pimp who was a suspect in a murder case. The team had to execute the warrant at a dingy club on Spring Street.

It was a deserted, industrial neighborhood where the manufacturing had left decades before; mostly tall, vacant loft buildings and ancient loading docks pimpled by bunches of half tires where the trailer-trucks backed up to the freight entrances. There was a slaughterhouse nearby. In the daytime, from two blocks away, you could see the blood running scarlet along the pavements, puddling in the curbs, smeared on the workers' long white coats, caked on anything you could touch.

The after-hours pimp bar was on the second floor above a dive that was open to the public. The whole block was owned by a businessman who rented almost exclusively to the mob.

The entrance to the upstairs after-hours club was protected by double steel doors. The setup was practically a prototype of how to run an illegal gin mill.

A vestibule fortress resembled the bailey of a medieval castle—as soon as you took down one iron-grated gate, another, with the two steel doors, confronted you. The defenses were designed to trap raiders, cops, between the two gates. But McCarthy and his men had to get inside.

"They called the doorman the 'manager,' but he was just an ape. All muscle, mean as hell. Sometimes, you could just bluff these big, dumb guys. But not this one. He was blocking our path. Since I was still in the early process of making points with the troops, I had to take the lead. Normally, I went in as the 'sledgeman,' the guy who swung the heavy hammer. But with steel doors like this place had, all the sledge would do is bounce off, right back in your face.

"We had to come on like *The Untouchables*. I got through the first gate, squeezed in, pried it apart. My men are right behind me, but if you can picture this, they're all still on the *other*

[85]

side. They can touch me through the grating, but they can't help me.

"I'm in there, between the two gates, just me and this monster—and he's bearing down on me, swinging a baseball bat, a real Louisville Slugger.

"I made a move to dive for his stomach and tackle him, but he made a better move, swerved, slammed me into the second steel gate; I was pinned.

"All at once I see him cock his bat over his shoulder like he's into his home-run swing. My head is the ball. My cops are behind me, trying to push through. But it just isn't working. And they're begging me to let them shoot this ape, crying like little kids. They all have their guns out; I'm the supervisor. I have to tell them to shoot.

"I go down into a crouch and use one arm to shield my head. Just as he swings, the bat kind of slides off my arm, just misses the elbow. If he'd planted himself a little better, he'd have crippled me.

"As he's coming out of his swing, I hooked his legs with my feet and kicked like hell. He fell down and I landed on top of him. The amazing part is, I'm still clutching the warrant. I took that piece of paper and shoved it right down his throat.

"Then, my cops come in."

While they were rolling around on the floor, the warrant was torn and became covered with blood. But the blood *wasn't* McCarthy's. He'd won—and no one had been shot. That became one more important moment in his long struggle to win his team's respect.

Through raid after raid, case after case, McCarthy was getting a riveting indoctrination into the Life. As he interrogated the johns and the other assorted repeat customers in the Vice underground, the consumers in the Life, he confiscated an impressive collection of both government and corporate IDs, credentials that had been issued by some of the Fortune 500 companies, places like Gulf + Western, Time Inc., most of the leading investment banks and brokerage houses on Wall Street, just about all of the big law firms.

At first, he thought that the Life appealed mainly to high-rolling associates of organized crime, but those wanna-be gangsters were just one faction, an important one but a small one, especially compared to the men and women in the Life who carried cards from all the right clubs and all the most expensive addresses.

The johns McCarthy arrested came from every imaginable profession: lawyers, teachers, judges, businessmen, rabbis, priests, even an occasional bishop. He traced one prominent pedophile to the main offices of the Archdiocese of New York. No one was immune from the compulsion of commercial, dangerous, and degraded sex.

The Life was reemerging after having been driven underground for better than a decade. The city itself was in a rebirth, reestablishing its place as the capital of the world. Real estate, commerce, political undercurrents, even crime were all on the upswing.

Nightlife in Manhattan was just coming back then, in the early 1970s. Joe Namath and the big sports celebrities probably started the rejuvenation of New York's club scene with places like Bachelors III—at least as far as the Vice cops were concerned.

The people in the Life pass through; clubs and bars change their names and their particular franchises, the details and the circumstances and the lewd minutiae of Vice have to be redefined for every generation, but the appetite itself, the craving and the inclination, remains a constant.

"When you run with that pack every night, begin at midnight, wear out by four or five o'clock, you burn out fast, become jaded. That trendy little club on the East Side that you couldn't wait to get to after work gets old fast. So you start looking for someplace new. Maybe a little wilder, a little cruder, a little more on the edge.

"Maybe just getting laid isn't good enough anymore. That's too tame. So you decide to go out and *pay* for it, make it a cash deal so that the girl becomes your property for those few minutes. She has to do anything you tell her to do. She's a woman who's different from anybody you've known before. Sex with her is the most risky, most exciting thing you've ever dreamed of. She's a whore. A hooker. A piece of meat that you went out and bought on the street. You can't get that back home. Not that edge.

"And, if you work in town, in Manhattan, that edge is no further away than the friendly neighborhood hooker on Seventh Avenue. The more wasted you become, the better she looks. And she might take you to a pimp bar that serves complimentary cocaine instead of matchbooks.

"It's exactly the same principle as drugs. You figure that your last high will never be as good as your next high. So you keep upping the ante. And you get drawn in, sucked in, a little further and further. It's gradual. But it's also cumulative, addictive. Maybe you don't even notice it. Then, bang, you've crossed the line without even realizing it.

"You're hooked: You can't make it through the day without some kind of fix—sex or cocaine or for people like me, like cops, danger.

"Believe me, I understand that kind of compulsive personality because I happen to be one.

"Plus, there is that intoxicating element of real danger. The pimps carry guns and knives; the whores are sexy-tough, little hustlers; and there are so many other kinds of characters around. In the Life you rub shoulders—and other body parts—with the kind of people you only ever see in the movies. Especially the women. That's what keeps drawing people to vice, people who should know better.

"I've seen a guy go into a porno store, look at a movie—a white male in his thirties, in a three-hundred-dollar suit, wearing a London Fog—right across from City Hall Park in the middle of New York. Then he comes out, drops his attaché case and starts masturbating right in public, jerking off, not even in a booth.

"I used to go into those places, the porno stores, with a search warrant, and the customer would be inside a peep show booth pleading, 'Please, officer, please, officer, just wait another minute, I'm not finished yet.' He'd be jerking off in there. 'Please, please let me finish.' Even his getting arrested had to wait."

No one was allowed to belittle a hooker around McCarthy. The days of the Pimp Team treating the hookers as disrespectfully as the pimps themselves ended. Plenty of old-time Vice cops didn't appreciate this approach, but McCarthy wasn't running for office. He sought results and was convinced that his methodology would succeed.

Eventually, as his own educational pursuits progressed, he even came up with the idea of developing personality inventories to test the women his men arrested. That began as an academic experiment, field research for McCarthy's master's thesis, but it soon became still another innovative intelligence-gathering tool.

"I became very comfortable in Vice. It's like being a good fly fisherman. I knew where to go in the pond to catch the biggest fish and I knew *how* to catch them. It became a matter of knowing how to troll the line.

"And all this information that I was getting, I was trying to make sense of it, use it, formulate it, allow it to determine my moves and my team's moves three, four weeks in advance. That was the only way to beat the people on the street, in the Life. Forget about outhustling them; they were and are and probably always will be the masters. All you could do was try to outplan them.

"As far as being in the Life went, if it happened in New York, the whores knew about it and if they knew about it, I could find it out.

"One thing I found out all about was sexual deviance. I understand it. I can predict it. I had this academic interest in psychology at the same time I was working in Vice. It was amazing how one pursuit fed into the other.

"I handed out my personality inventories to every whore I could find. Here I was, supposed to be a Pimp cop, but I was actually more interested in them as people—badly abused people. Cops being cops, they thought I was the craziest psycho in the world. And maybe I was. That kind of reputation was useful, too. I would do crazy things because I enjoyed that identity.

"I used to dance in all the black bars that we hit. When they had music on, I'd sing. The black guys would all be dancing too and I'd say, 'You call that dancing?' Then I'd show them my stuff. The pimps couldn't believe that a white guy could dance like I did, like a maniac. But I learned all those steps back at Power Memorial on the West Side. The whores would watch me and say, 'Man, you must fuck good.' And I'd just get this little smile on my face and nod my head really slowly. Any cop who says that Vice isn't one of the funniest, bawdiest, loosest places in the world to be, along with being one of the most depressing, of course, is full of it. Every night was a party.

"Then we would move in for a captive audience, literally. Within minutes we usually had every person in the place up against the bar railing with shotguns pointed at them. That was how we always took down a tough spot—scatterguns. And it was all a bluff. Only once in my entire police career was I anywhere near a shotgun that went off, and that turned out to be a big mistake.

"But the guys in the bars, of course, never knew any of that. They didn't know what to make of me."

Neither did most of the other policemen in Manhattan Vice. The one thing they were sure of was that McCarthy was the most uncoplike cop any of them had ever seen. He approached his job as a vocation; there was a decidedly priestly zeal—as well as rigidity—in his efforts to clean up vice in Manhattan and in his curiosity to discern how it had gotten so dirty in the first place. Telling "McCarthy stories," "Mother stories," became an insider's passion among the Vice detectives. Respect for his methods, which seemed odd at first, especially in the intellectually moribund NYPD, was painfully slow in coming. But it did come. After his first year in Vice, there were very few cops working that beat in New York who hadn't heard of "Mother."

"To make a collar we had to witness a sex act or sexual performance, or we had to be solicited for sex. And the rule was that we couldn't get naked or actually have sex with the girls. If you did, then it was all over. That was what always separated the real johns from the cops. But nobody who ever worked for me got in any trouble. If you ever touched a girl on me, even once, you were gone. I was Mother and I had to back it up every time.

"It took a cast-iron stomach to sit through some of those sex club acts. One of the more famous 'performers' used to be able get up on the stage, bend over, and stick a hot dog up her ass. Then she'd blow, shoot it out, and hit a guy in the third row.

"I used to have to send undercovers in there because all the hookers knew me. I used to coach the new cops: 'Don't sit in the last row. Don't sit in the last row.' They were all so afraid to sit in the last row, because she used to blow the guys in the last row. She'd come down off the stage and say, 'I'm gonna get all those gay little boys in the back.' There was no place to escape. That woman happens to be an upstanding Jesus freak today.

"As a cop, you were there to watch the performance, but in addition to watching the performance, you know that a prostitute's gonna come up and say 'I'll give you a blow-job for fifty dollars.'

"You're gonna lock her up for prostitution. You can say to the bartender, 'Look, is there some place I can get laid?' He says to you, 'Yeah, there's a girl back there.' That's the way it works. The cop is undercover from the outset. He can end up arresting the girl and the bartender. That's an easy collar.

"Our job was to get the evidence and get it safely and be able later to make accurate police reports and, if it ever got into court, testify. That was a lot of paperwork. We wasted hours and hours preparing cases that would proceed two steps beyond us and then get blown out, fixed. But it was all part of the game.

"The cops have a saying that the job is not on the level. That it's a game and you just play along. But the job can be on any level that you want it to be on. And, if it's only a game, then nobody should ever get hurt. Tell that to a dead cop."

The typical Times Square area whorehouse of the early 1970s was located in a dreary storefront, masquerading as a "massage parlor" or "dating service" or "escort bureau" or even a topless bar. Sometimes, there might be a peep show or X-rated theater or "adult bookstore" located on the ground floor. Without exception, though, real sex would be available upstairs or "in the back."

The interior of the storefront might consist of a sitting room—a few folding chairs with a table and Polaroid shots of the "hostesses." Behind that were the "session rooms"—dirty, bare-walled cubicles, equipped with little slabs of plywood, covered by foam rubber or paper or, in the more expensive places, sheets. And there would always be a plastic waste paper basket, filled with rolled-up pieces of tissue—with used condoms in the tissues. The women who accepted money for sex in these cubicles almost always had three things in common: They were young, battered-looking, and silent. That was the low end of sex-for-pay.

"The whores might be waiting out in the sitting rooms, lined up against the walls like kids at a dance. You'd come in and see them smoking or watching television or picking from some greasy bag of french fries. You walked in there and picked one out.

"Don't ask me what the attraction was. Maybe she looked like somebody you used to know, or you liked her tits or she happened to smile back at you. I've seen thousands of them, busted them, interviewed them, allowed them to cry on my shoulder;

I even made some of them fill out surveys for my college papers if I happened to be doing something on prostitution. And I dearly love sex—but I never ran into a single one of them that even made me hard. Ninety percent or more of the attraction has to be inside your own head. Up close they are just sad, pathetic, exploited human beings.

"After you paid this old bitch, the madam, then you could rap with one of the girls for a few minutes and then, just about as fast as you could get your pants down, you'd be allowed to screw her for maybe nine minutes. Any longer and they'd ask you to pay for two sessions.

"Later, there were fancier places like Plato's Retreat, but that was one of a kind. By then, it was like a tourist shrine. The real whores didn't even work there. Another variation were the bathhouses. You might see a fountain and some running water in there, but it was still the same thing—cheap, hollow, depressing sex.

"There was one bar we used to hit that was a real hangout for Wall Street types. I don't think any of the johns in there had an income under a hundred thousand dollars, back when that was serious money. It was called the Wild West, over on Thirty-fifth Street. They liked to tell the customers they would 'give them a little heat.'

"As soon as you sat down at one of the tables, a girl would walk over and sort of straddle your lap. Then, while she's sitting on your lap, after a few minutes, you would get this warm rush on your thigh—'heat,' urine; that was their act. Water sports. The girl would piss all over you. That joint used to pack them in, believe me. The johns who didn't want to be pissed on knew enough not to sit down, because as soon as you did, you were asking for it.

"There was another whorehouse called The Episode, where each girl would do eighty tricks a day. After a week, you looked like you had ridden a horse from here to California. They were bowlegged. The better whores, however, all had some kind of a gimmick.

"The madams taught them—the trick is to get a guy so excited about anticipating sex that when you touch him, he goes off right away, explodes. That only took them thirty seconds. It meant less actual, physical exertion to the transaction. That's more efficient for them. Or, you try to do only oral sex. Less wear and tear.

"As the price goes up, the conditions change somewhat. A high-priced call girl is attractive, has some sense of society, can make a few sentences of conversation before the client pants like a dog and, most importantly, she can charge triple the price. But eventually, when her innocence and attractiveness start to diminish, she'll have to increase her sexual activity to make the same amount of money and that will accelerate her physical disintegration. Ultimately, even the whores who started out charging five-hundred dollars a night will arrive in the herd of the streetwalkers—those ambulating jars of pus.

"In Vice you learn that the definition of a whore is a person who takes green paper from white men and then gives them permission to spit on her—or him—with semen. That's what a prostitute is: a receptacle for white men's semen. Most johns are white, middle-aged men in business attire. It isn't always white men, of course, but most of the time they're white. And about half the time or more, the prostitutes aren't. The johns come from that class of buttoned-down suburban office workers. Sex is an irretractable compulsion with them. They are misinformed and naive, ignorant of the danger, of the jeopardy. But, believe it or not, AIDS hasn't even slowed it down that much.

"There are many different kinds of prostitutes, but regardless of how glamorous they appear to be, no matter how much they charge, no body is made to take that kind of work. You can't get laid twenty, thirty, thirty-five times a day. You just can't stand up to it.

"Every whore I ever arrested powdered her nose. You get rid of prostitutes by getting rid of cocaine. If there was no cocaine, you'd have no pimps. If you had no pimps, you'd have no whores. The cycle feeds on itself. This is basic: A woman or a man sells his or her body to get the money to afford the coke.

That might sound facile, but it happens to be true.

"You deal with all sorts of drug addicts in Vice. Without a doubt, the saddest ones are the prostitutes. They're all losers. They end up trying to sell bodies that are covered with filthy scabs, blown-out junkies with sunken veins. I've seen people scratch their scabs and almost bore open holes into their arms.

"You pick up their tongue and underneath it will be lacerated with canker sores. They inject the dope under their tongues to try to clean up their arms when they have to go to their probation officer.

"In the gay bars—which were worse, more wide-open, more likely to feature sexual performances that involved most of the audience—you rarely had the stereotypical old hag madam. That's where they called them managers. Always men.

"The Beloved Disciple was a converted church in Lower Manhattan. You passed through the confessional booth, gave the password and proceeded down a flight of stairs—like descending into Hades. That passageway opened onto the dance floor of an after-hours club.

"At night, even outside, people walked around almost naked. They would wear cowboy's chaps and leather hats, but nothing else. Their asses and dicks were hanging out.

"In another place where we were trying to serve a warrant, I went in alone, undercover, in leather, and had my cops dressed up with electric suits and whips. But they never let them in.

"Gray leather was chic. If I wore that jacket, I could go anywhere. The club is packed. The only spot available at the bar is in front of the flap door that the bartender uses. I take up my position, intending to let the raiding party in later.

"Urine was the fetish here, too. Like a gay version of the Wild West club. The only way you could avoid getting urine in your drink was to order a can of beer. The guy next to me paid thirty-five dollars for a 'sports bourbon,' which is bourbon and urine, and he kept complaining that it was diluted. Too much bourbon.

"I'm sipping my beer. One of the other customers comes up

and grabs me by my balls. He says, 'I'm bashful.'

"'If you're bashful, I don't want to meet your brother.'

"Then, he spits in my ear and bites me on my ear lobe and rubs his hands all over my chest and says, 'Ooooh! I just got back from Caracas. I'm a steward with Pan Am. All these men. They're exhausting me.' He's rubbing his hands all over my chest. He now has my shirt out of my pants.

"I tell the guy, 'Listen, I'm waiting for my boyfriend and I really don't want him to make a scene. He's very jealous. I would love to meet you. Is it possible that I could meet you some other time? But if I'm seen with you now, there's gonna be a scene.'

"I stayed there for two hours by myself. I would say that I had my balls squeezed about eight times, guys trying to kiss me, spit on my neck, but I was able to psyche myself up to handle it. Most cops couldn't.

"They were all dropping down and blowing each other, but that wasn't the collar I was looking to make. So I left. Just another shift in Manhattan Vice.

"Before I left I had to use the bathroom. I knew that was going to be a mistake. But I had to go.

"I try to use the urinal and there's a guy sitting on it. I guess I stared. He says, 'What's the matter with you?' He wanted me to piss on him. There's a guy defecating in the toilet and another guy is standing over him, while the guy who is blowing him is getting screwed in the ass and there's three guys outside masturbating, watching.

"I left the bathroom in a big hurry.

"The majority of them were white; ninety-five percent had unbelievably muscular bodies. Big truck drivers, football players, S-and-M people. And a lot of them were ex-convicts because there's so much homosexuality in the prisons. They just get to like it. To them—and some of the ex-cons told me this—it was good sex without all the bullshit conversation you had to go through with a woman trying to get laid. They'll tell you that women are a pain in the ass. You gotta date them, feed them, and hope.

"I couldn't get over the anonymity of it. They don't even say hello or goodbye. They don't introduce themselves. A guy will blow you and you won't even get his name.

"All the bathrooms had glory holes. You could stick your dick through the wall and another guy on the other side would blow you. There's a hole in the wall of every toilet.

"The next week we arrive and we don't get in. So the next time we go in with a warrant. We get in then. But no dope or booze. The place has been sanitized.

"I take the manager in the back room and he says to me, very sweetly, 'Sergeant, you got your warrant signed on October 24, at 6:24 P.M. hours. Right? We knew all about it.'

"My warrant reads: October 24, 18:24 hours. It's the same date and time.

"You have ten days to execute that warrant from the minute that the judge signs it. Which meant that the manager or someone had access to the sealed court records. That's a very serious breach of police security.

"I tell him that I will pay him ten thousand dollars if he tells me who gave up the warrant. Who was the corrupt person who gave up the info about the warrant?

"'Sergeant, you're making a big mistake if you think it's only one person.'

"He was right about that. We traced it down and there was a state senator, a district attorney, and a court officer involved. All of them were homosexuals who knew people connected to that club. I found that out unofficially. Couldn't make a single arrest.

"The Anvil kept a string of llamas downstairs; you could make it with the llama. They still do that.

"The main floor show was 'the master.' He was a giant black guy, I think he was an ex-pro football player, and all he wore was this big, metal-studded harness that looked like a heavyweight fighter's championship belt. The master started out by climbing a pole that was in the middle of the dance floor.

"He'd crack his penis against the studded belt until he had an orgasm. He did that every hour on the hour. Then, he'd look around the dance floor, select some lucky patron and put

[97]

Crisco all over the guy's ass. Then the master would stick his hand up the guy's ass all the way to his elbow, and end it by picking the guy up with one arm, walking him around the room, banging his head against the ceiling.

"Same show every night. People would line up, sticking money in the master's face, begging him to pick them.

"One night when we were there the master pulled his arm out of the guy's butt and his rectum prolapsed. It came right out on the master's arm. I thought I was witnessing a murder. But he survived. A week later that guy was back in the club, looking for the master."

Conventional cop wisdom still maintained that whores and their pimps were essentially free-lance operators. It denigrated both the job of the Pimp Squad and the value of any intelligence to be gathered there. McCarthy's team finally exploded those myths along with several others. Naturally, the people with vested interests in maintaining the old way of thinking, including corrupt cops and the pimps who paid them off, became furious with McCarthy; but they had to get in line.

The mob Families were also wondering what was happening as one after another of their most lucrative houses gave way to one of McCarthy's sledges.

Both inside and outside the department, questions were beginning to be asked. The underworld had been paying out top dollar, for years, to generations of cops who doubled and tripled their legitimate incomes by making sure that the sex clubs were left alone or "protected." But for some reason, the Vice team headed by McCarthy hadn't gotten the message.

TWELVE

A *Corrupt Cop* is the most definable person in the whole world. The people in the Life know exactly what to expect from a corrupt cop. He has a standing invitation. Everybody wants to know him.

MOTHER'S MAXIM

███

One night around eight o'clock, just before McCarthy was getting ready to unlock the door at 137 Centre Street and report upstairs to Vice, he heard someone calling his name from the quiet darkness of a doorway near the side of the building.

He knew that the municipal offices would be practically deserted by that time of night, and the sidewalk behind him was nearly empty too. His gun was jammed into the small of his back, between the waistband of his dungarees and shirt; there was a lightweight jacket over that.

Before even acknowledging the voice, before looking in the direction from which it had come, McCarthy moved his arm and hand around under the jacket to get a grip on the handle of his .38 detective special. His team had been busting pimps nonstop the past few months, serving a record number of warrants, slowing down Vice business all over Manhattan and, in general, earning an unforgiving reputation in the Life. Sure as hell, he reasoned, somebody was here either to offer him a payoff or try to take him out for good. Either way it would be a problem. McCarthy was only in suspense about one thing—would it turn out to be another cop or a bad guy?

[99]

Then, the voice piped up again: "Sergeant McCarthy; Sergeant William McCarthy." He said it a little louder this time; there was traffic on the street and the noise from it was beginning to build.

Staring into the blackness, he waited. This was the nervous time. Suddenly, he was very scared.

"Captain Gussman wants me to talk to you." Then the voice reeled off both McCarthy's badge number and his confidential police ID number, a series of random digits meant for internal security use only.

He now knew that the voice had to belong to another policeman or to someone with access to the most sensitive files at One Police Plaza. So it appeared that another cop was approaching him after all. They had given him six months since the date of his appointment to Vice; now it would be time for McCarthy to take a stand or get on the pad. He was sure that the "reach" was about to be made.

"I want to see both hands first," McCarthy called back, as he carefully took his gun out from under the jacket.

Two large, pinkish hands appeared, slowly coming out of the shadows cast by the overhead street lights.

"That's fine, right there," McCarthy said. "Now, just hold them up. Come forward one step."

As the Vice cop moved in, he saw that the nails on each hand—big, fleshy masculine hands—were neatly manicured and buffed. Whoever it was, it didn't look as though he'd done any serious work in a very long time.

Just before beginning to frisk him, McCarthy pulled the man out into the uncertain light. He was tall, he had at least a head on McCarthy. Their eyes locked on one another. In that instant, McCarthy jumped back a full step. Focusing on the face before him—a disconcertingly familiar face—McCarthy couldn't conceal his surprise. It was an inspector whom he had known fairly well over the years. Not a friend, by any means, but an officer whose savvy and cunning he had come to hold in high regard.

McCarthy hadn't seen him recently, however. He'd been

transferred to work out of the first deputy commissioner's office in the Puzzle Palace. In fact, no one really knew what he had been up to, although departmental gossip linked him with some secret offshoot of internal affairs. This guy was from the wrong side of Foley Square, as far as McCarthy was concerned.

The inspector smiled like a hungry man who was just about to tuck the napkin into his shirt. Then he indicated that they both should remain away from the light, on the side of the building. McCarthy immediately complied.

"Captain Gussman sends his regards," the inspector began. Then he stopped, looked quizzically at McCarthy and continued. "He also said for me to tell you that no one would be sending you out for any cigarettes." The inspector waited for some reaction from McCarthy, but the Vice cop refused to give anything away. "He assured me that you would know what they meant."

"Gussman was right, I do," McCarthy answered in an unusually clipped tone. "What's with the cloak and dagger stuff?"

At least he knew that this whole thing somehow had Gussman's seal of approval, and he did trust Kenny Gussman. That was a relief.

The inspector, a craggy Irish bull elephant with a white crew cut and rippling rolls of loose skin that cascaded down a sloping forehead, brought his face down level with McCarthy's.

"Best not to give any of the big ears a chance to overhear what I'm about to tell you," he said. "You've been making people take notice of you, lad." There was animation, but no detectable emotion in his voice.

"Is that good or bad?" McCarthy asked.

"Ah, it's all in one's point of view, isn't it?"

They were both silent for a moment. Then, the older man added, "I'm sure you're aware of the fact that your fan club has been very active."

"Does that leave me dead or alive?"

"That's your choice," the inspector said.

McCarthy didn't understand, not at first. His face became a

little more questioning than he intended it to be.

"Let me simplify it for you." The inspector was reading him quite accurately. McCarthy had to give him that.

"There's still a Sergeant's Club, bigger than ever, which you are no doubt familiar with, and they would love to see you join. And so would we. But..." he paused like a vaudevillian making certain that his timing was impeccable, "but, you haven't exactly been out soliciting an invitation. Or have you? No bullshit now, lad."

It was as though the inspector spoke in code. Old school, very old school. McCarthy respected that, knew where he was coming from. The "Sergeant's Club" referred to one of the pads, or bribery schemes, that the Knapp Commission had been struggling so singlemindedly to destroy. The reform crusade had not worked, not entirely. The New York City Police Department had been corrupt for hundreds of years; Knapp had been in business for slightly less than three.

McCarthy wasn't a member of any Sergeant's Club; he never had been. Abhorring corrupt cops as he did, he had distanced himself from a large segment of the department. Working in an area as potentially lucrative as Vice had only served to make his refusal to partake in any of the payoffs that much more notable.

"If you talked to Gussman, then you already know I'm not on a pad," McCarthy said. "And *that's* no bullshit. So why should the first deputy commissioner have any questions about my motives?"

"He's a cautious man," the inspector answered. "We've seen hard-chargers like you before. Some of them turned out to be charging so hard just to increase their price. But you're right. Gussman vouched for you. Among others."

"Why come to me?"

"Target of opportunity, my lad," he replied, sliding the phrase off his tongue like a reptile shedding its skin. "You can either keep on doing what you're doing, which is fine with us, of course, or you can make yourself infinitely more useful.

Which also happens to be the considered opinion of Saint Paul. He stood up for you too."

So Paul Delise, Serpico's mentor, was also in on it. McCarthy thought back to the night Saint Paul had tapped his own telephone, monitoring all of his conversations. How many other nights had he been listening?

"We need you inside," the inspector said directly, "as deep undercover as you can get."

"How?" McCarthy was already known as Mother. He had a reputation and he lived up to it. "People know who I am, how I operate. I haven't exactly been quiet about it. And I doubt that they would buy a flip-flop at this point."

"I wouldn't be so sure about that," the inspector said. "Things change; a man like you can begin developing more refined tastes, new friends. That all costs money."

"You want me to get lost in the Life?"

"Do it gradually, but not too gradually. Go as far and as fast as you can. Make it look good, but plausible. Hit the bars, the after-hours clubs, chase the whores. Do all the things that a sergeant faced with those temptations might normally do." The inspector cleared his throat for effect. "Then, begin to let people on the street get the idea that you're prepared to listen to reason. Square a few beefs for certain people, get them owing you favors—the right kind of favors. Let them know that you intend to collect. If I know them, they'll just think that you played out the string as an honest cop for as long as you could and finally decided to do what a thousand other guys have done: cash in and go for the fast money. Why should you be any different?"

"And after the 'gradual,' what then?"

The inspector was obviously ready for this, the script had already been written. "Then, if it ever comes to that, you will have a very convenient blowup with your good friend and superior officer, Kenneth Gussman, who, God bless him, will begin to very publicly suspect that you are on the take. He will accuse you in front of a carefully selected group of witnesses of our choosing. At that point, you punch Gussman in the mouth and begin acting like you're guilty as sin.

"Unless I miss my guess, the suitors will start crooning at your window. You'll be irresistible. A disgruntled Vice cop, with a hard-on against all of his old friends. The bent-noses should fall right in line."

McCarthy just listened. The whole point of the proposal that was being thrown at him amounted to: Let's put cops in handcuffs. The game they were playing would eventually involve the highest level of intrigue that NYPD had ever known. Counterespionage within the department. Intrigue on top of intrigue. And they wanted him to become a major player in it.

The inspector continued. "We yank you out of Vice, under a very dark cloud, and assign you to a patrol district, still as a sergeant. Use your head, under those conditions how long do you think it would take for someone to invite you to join the club?"

"Probably until about the second shift," McCarthy said, smiling.

"Precisely. My orders to approach you come directly from the first deputy commissioner. It's up to you. Think it over. But don't *talk* it over. Except with your wife. If she's against it, a woman can make your life a living hell. I know." He looked like he did.

McCarthy's head was spinning like the little ball on a roulette wheel.

The old man handed him a small piece of paper, folded once. "Call this number by twelve noon tomorrow," he said. "All you have to do is tell us one word, 'yes' or 'no'; we'll take it from there. If it's 'no,' you won't be hearing from us again. Sleep on it, lad." And then he left. No handshake, no parting words.

McCarthy couldn't concentrate at all that night. He kept weighing the pros and cons. They were asking him to assume what amounted to a new identity. While it might be worth it as a career move, the toll on his family would be tremendous. He already knew what Millie thought about cops who took money. Her ad-